About the Book . . .

"This is an extraordinary account of a man seeking inner peace and total commitment to God. . . . a fine portrait of cloistered life, a beautifully written account of one man's soul-searching." —*Publishers Weekly*

". . . a unique and personal document. What emerges is the baring of a very gifted writer's soul. Nouwen's devastating frankness in his soul-searching is a great aid in helping the reader identify with him as he opens his soul to his spiritual master."

—Bro. Patrick Hart in *America*

"Reading this book is a wonderful experience. *The Genesee Diary* is a superb report about joy and God and Henri Nouwen. The power of Nouwen's diary lies in its capacity to shatter such favorite illusions and return them to us in truer form." —*Cross Currents*

"This unsparingly honest book is inspirational in the best sense. It inspires confidence in the author; it inspires one to imitation without false expectation; it inspires trust in ancient ways of judgment and prayer which the trend think to be outmoded. And it is packed with comments, descriptions, and incidents which are delightful and instructive." —*Our Sunday Visitor*

"For easygoing reflection and fresh insight into the monastic life, Nouwen's diary is tops. He records his moods and observations during seven months as a 'temporary Trappist' and leaves us with a realistic look at the power and grace of the monastic vocation—a vocation which does not solve all problems in our life, but helps one to praise God with new vigor. Nouwen emerges with a new strength to deal with the human condition, and we can profit from his pilgrimage." —*The Christian Century*

THE GENESEE DIARY

The Genesee Diary:
Report from a Trappist Monastery

Henri J. M. Nouwen

COMPLETE AND UNABRIDGED

DARTON · LONGMAN + TODD

This edition published in Great Britain in 1995 by
Darton, Longman and Todd Ltd
1 Spencer Court
140–142 Wandsworth High Street
London SW18 4JJ

Reprinted 1999 and 2003
This edition 2008

First published in the USA in 1976 by Doubleday,
a division of Bantam Doubleday Dell Publishing Group, Inc.
1540 Broadway, New York, NY 10036

A catalogue record for this book is available
from the British Library

ISBN-10 0–232–52729–6
ISBN-13 978–0–232–52729–2

Printed and bound in Great Britain by
The Cromwell Press, Trowbridge, Wiltshire

To all contemplative men and women
who by their commitment to unceasing
prayer offer us hope in the midst
of a troubled world.

ACKNOWLEDGMENTS

Many friends have helped me make the decision to publish this diary. I want to express my deep gratitude to Ellie Drury, Louis Dupré, Bob Lifton, Mu-Gak, Eric Olson, Colin Williams, Richard White, Arnold Wolf, and Phil Zaeder for the time and the attention they have given to the writings of which this diary is a selection. Without their encouragement, I would have never been able to follow through with the suggestion that my diary might be of interest to more than a small circle of friends.

I owe a special word of thanks to Dorothy Holman who was the first to make me think about the possibility of publication when she said, "This is the most unselfconscious writing you have done. Maybe you should have it printed exactly because you didn't write it with that purpose in mind." That same unselfconsciousness, however, was the cause of many linguistic and stylistic weaknesses. I am very grateful to Stephen Leahy, Bob Werner, and John Mogabgab for the care with which they corrected the manuscript.

Finally, I want to express my appreciation for the editorial help of Bob Heller and the secretarial assistance of Pat Murray Kelly, Cyndy Halverson, Katie Hicks, and Claire Mattern.

CONTENTS

INTRODUCTION

My desire to live for seven months in a Trappist Monastery, not as a guest but as a monk, did not develop overnight. It was the outcome of many years of restless searching. While teaching, lecturing, and writing about the importance of solitude, inner freedom, and peace of mind, I kept stumbling over my own compulsions and illusions. What was driving me from one book to another, one place to another, one project to another? What made me think and talk about "the reality of the Unseen" with the seriousness of one who had seen all that is real? What was turning my vocation to be a witness to God's love into a tiring job? These questions kept intruding themselves into my few unfilled moments and challenging me to face my restless self. Maybe I spoke more about God than with him. Maybe my writing about prayer kept me from a prayerful life. Maybe I was more concerned about the praise of men and women than the love of God. Maybe I was slowly becoming a prisoner of people's expectations instead of a man liberated by divine promises. Maybe . . . It was not all that clear, but I realized that I would only know by stepping back and allowing the hard questions to touch me even if they hurt. But stepping back was not so easy. I had succeeded in surrounding myself with so many classes to prepare, lectures to give, articles to finish, people to meet, phone calls to make, and letters to answer, that I had come quite close to believing that I was indispensible.

When I took a closer look at this I realized that I was caught in a web of strange paradoxes. While complaining about too many demands, I felt uneasy when none were made. While speaking about the burden of letter writing, an empty mailbox made me sad. While fretting about tiring lecture tours, I felt disappointed when there were no invitations. While speaking nostalgically about an empty desk, I feared the day on which that would come true. In short: while desiring to be alone, I was frightened of being left alone. The more I became aware of these paradoxes, the more I started to see how much I had indeed fallen in love with my own compulsions and illusions, and how much I needed to step back and wonder, "Is there a quiet stream underneath the fluctuating affirmations and rejections of my little world? Is there a still point where my life is anchored and from which I can reach out with hope and courage and confidence?"

While realizing my growing need to step back, I knew that I could never do it alone. It seems that the crucial decisions and the great experiences of life require a guide. The way to "God alone" is seldom traveled alone. For me there was little, if any, question about the need for guidance. At first it was very unclear what exactly that would mean. But my own travels on the roads of the U.S.A. as well as on the paths of the spiritual search had slowly prepared me for an answer.

About ten years ago, while on a long trip from Miami to Topeka, I stopped at the Trappist Abbey of Gethsemani in Kentucky, in the hope of finding someone with whom I could talk. When the guestmaster learned that I had studied psychology and was at the point of joining the faculty of a psychology department, he said with a happy twinkle in his eyes: "But we Trappists have a psychologist too! I will ask him to visit you." A little later Father John Eudes Bamberger walked into the guest room.

Very soon I knew that I had met a rare and very convincing person. John Eudes listened to me with care and interest, but also with a deep conviction and a clear vision; he
gave me much time and attention but did not allow me to
waste a minute; he left me fully free to express my feelings and thoughts but did not hesitate to present his own;
he offered me space to deliberate about choices and to
make decisions but did not withhold his opinion that some
choices and decisions were better than others; he let me
find my own way but did not hide the map that showed
the right direction. In our conversation, John Eudes
emerged not only as a listener but also as a guide, not
only as a counselor but also as a director. It did not take
me long to realize that this was the man I had needed so
badly.

John Eudes' own history, in which both psychology and
theology play a major role, offered so many connections
with my own story that I had a vital sense of God's guidance in our encounter. His medical and psychiatric training, his theological education and monastic formation and
his far-reaching experiences ranging from his duty in the
U. S. Navy to his roles as infirmarian and novice master
seemed to reflect many of my own endeavors, aspirations,
and fantasies.

This unusual combination of differences and similarities
offered the graceful context in which spiritual direction
could grow and continue to grow It is therefore not surprising that during my many subsequent visits to Gethsemani I came to know John Eudes not only as a very insightful but also as a very compassionate spiritual guide.

After a three-year stay in Europe, during which my
contact with John Eudes was minimal, I heard that he
had been elected Abbot of the Abbey of the Genesee in
upstate New York. My first visit there gave me the idea
that maybe in the near future I could break away from
my work, explore my compulsions and illusions, and live
as a temporary monk under the regular guidance of John
Eudes. I vividly remember my hesitation in formulating
this idea. I was so aware of the unusual nature of my

desire to be a temporary Trappist, that I didn't expect much more than a smile saying, "We enter here for a lifetime, not for a sabbatical." But the "no" which I had expected did not come. John Eudes was open to the idea and said, "Although our monastic community does not admit temporary members, I will think about your desire, discuss it with the monks, and see if we can make an exception." A half year later a letter came with the good news that I had been "voted in," and that I could come when I was ready for it. Finally on June 1, 1974, after a lot of desk cleaning, I flew to Rochester, New York, to live as a Trappist monk for seven months, and on Pentecost, June 2, I started to write the notes that found their final form in this diary.

CHAPTER ONE

JUNE

A Stranger in Paradise

JUNE

Sunday, 2

Thanks be to God that I am here! When Walter met me
last night at the Rochester Airport and drove me through
the darkening Genesee valley to the Trappist Monastery, I
had a deep sense of gratitude. I knew it was a good decision to interrupt my life for seven months and join the
thirty monks who had impressed me so much when I
visited them two years ago.

When we drove up to the buildings the splendid red
sky had become sparkling dark. Walter showed me my
room in the center of a small corridor where the monks
had their cells. It was silent. . . . The abbot, John
Eudes, had sent a card with Walter to wish me welcome,
and on my desk I found a friendly note from the prior,
Father Stephen, telling me that breakfast would be on the
table between 3 and 5 A.M. In the dark I found the chapel
and prayed.

How much reason to say thanks, how much reason to
pray that God will turn my heart to him and set me free
by his love. Seven months: The only feeling I have is that
it will be too short, too temporary, too experimental. But
today is Pentecost, and Christmas is far away.

Back in my "cell" I unpacked my suitcase and was surprised by the collection of books I had decided to take with me: A Spanish Bible, the works of Saint John of the Cross, a history of the United States, a book about common weeds, and the novel, *Zen and the Art of Motorcycle Maintenance*. Maybe this selection is the expression of my unconscious fear that I might get bored in a Trappist monastery.

Monday, 3

I met Brother Elias, a hermit of the Abbey. Brother Christian, the cook with whom I had developed a friendship during an earlier visit, showed me the way through the woods and introduced me to this remarkable man. During the twenty minutes we talked, Elias told me practically everything I needed to hear. He told me how the changes in the often rough climate were good—"goo-o-o-d," he said—because they deepened his longing for God. As the storms made him wish for gentle winds, the clouds for the sun, dryness for rains, so his heart learned to yearn for God and take nothing for granted. "What is so good about this part of the country," he said, "is that it makes you realize that áll good things are gifts of God—when the sun is always shining you forget that it is God's gift, and you don't pay attention any more." While he said this, his small round bearded face with happy eyes seemed to become transparent.

His directness and simplicity were beautiful. While speaking about his love for the Lord, he said, "When I get excited about the Lord, my temptation is to go out and tell everyone about him—but that I shouldn't do—I should stay here and pray." Looking me right in the face with his great eyes he added, "Don't worry about how to speak about the Lord. When you allow him to enter into your heart, he will give you words."

I needed to hear this because I still *was* worrying about

lack of time for study and reading and about courses after this time was over. Was it really wise to interrupt my work for this simple life? How would it help me to be a better teacher? I knew these were the wrong questions. I knew that theology needed to be born out of prayer, but Brother Elias had to say it again so I would not forget it.

We also talked about Thomas Merton. Elias was able to criticize him in the form of a compliment. "He was a good writer—his books are very good—the little bit of solitude he had, he talked about very well." I knew how right he was. Merton's deep desire for solitude had been in constant tension with his gregarious personality. There were always many people around him, if not physically then through mail and books. And he loved it. But until the last days of his life he kept dreaming about a hermitage where he could be alone with God. During his travels through India he wrote about a possible hermitage in Alaska. The tension between his great desire for solitude and his deep compassion for so many people made Merton the writer he was, and Brother Elias knew it.

Brother Elias showed us his few vegetable plants and explained that he did not need drinking water since there was enough of it in the vegetables he ate. I asked about his discipline. He said, "I rise at 2 A.M., do the exercises of the Canadian Army to build my muscles up, and then I do Yoga." During the night hours he prays and takes care of his different needs—small needs but real ones—clothes, food, and the maintenance of his little hut. Early in the morning he leaves the hermitage and goes to his carpentry shop to make furniture for the new church. In the afternoon he studies and meditates. Around 7 P.M. he goes to bed to be ready for a fresh start the next day.

We looked around his little hermitage. A single room with one corner sectioned off as a little chapel. Two tables with books, a bed hooked up against the wall, and a small mat for his Yoga. He showed it with joy. He asked my blessing, said how happy he was to meet me, and kept waving good-bye while we walked away.

Tuesday, 4

Today was "hermit day," which means that you are free from 6 A.M. to 4:30 P.M. to do what you want. It was a good day for me. I slept most of the morning after a walk through the humid fields. My sleep was deep and heavy, as it has been since I came here. I seem to have many "double dreams." Dreams about dreaming, dreams about waking up, dreams about sleeping in, etc.—I must be very tired, but I seem to be catching up. Nothing unexpected.

The continuous silence is a real healing experience for me. The monks mostly communicate in sign language. Only when the subject gets too complicated for their fingers do they invite each other to the rooms that are reserved for necessary conversation.

It was fun making my own lunch. I burned my thumb while trying to bring some water to a boil. John Eudes, noticing my attempts to remain silent with a hurting hand, told me to stick my finger in the butter which I did. The pain was soon gone.

Wednesday, 5

After Lauds—the communal morning prayer at 5 A.M.—Brother Anthony put me to work in the bakery on the "hot-bread line." With baseball-like gloves, I picked up the hot bread—first brown bread, then white bread, then raisin bread—and put them on racks to be pushed away to the "cooling room." The good-natured Brother Christian did the same, and he always makes things look easier. When I saw the hundreds of loaves move in my direction I panicked. But Brother Christian smiled and took a few of "my loaves" when he noticed that I could not keep up.

Meanwhile, I meditated on the sentence "With sweat on your brow shall you eat your bread" (Gen. 3:19). Bread and sweat had never been closer together in my life.

Had a good talk with John Eudes. I told him how I had enjoyed my stay so far, how much I liked the community, and how the whole experience seemed a luxury. He not only didn't deny it but said that the sole idea of the monastic life was that of creating a life-long vacation! "You can't do that on your own, so we form communities and we experience all of life as a gift of God—that is why praise is so central—praise for God's gifts." I said cautiously that maybe I would feel differently after a few months and that there might be more tensions than I had foreseen, but he said, "No, no—you'll like it more, the longer you are here. The Cistercians always considered the monastery as a little paradise on earth. Read St. Bernard." I frankly had not expected so much affirmation of my good feelings but was the more grateful for it. The rest of the time we talked about books on the spirituality of the desert fathers (Hesychasm). John Eudes will be a good guide for the study of this tradition. He gave very helpful suggestions. We went to the library and selected a few books to start with.

Thursday, 6

This has been a workman's day. I worked at the hot-bread line with Brother James, the postulant, who sits in choir in such a devout way that you think that any moment his head will fall off. A fine man. Son of a dairy farmer in Rochester. During the break between the brown and the white bread, he told me that his father no longer worked the farm but wanted one of his sons to take over. James did it for a while, then entered the Trappists four months ago. Now one of his brothers is giving it a try. He said he had enough brothers to try it out, but nobody seemed ready yet to buy the farm. When, after two hours' work, the good-smelling raisin bread came down on the conveyor belt, James turned around, looked at me and said with a big smile, "When I am all through with this I could eat a whole loaf of it."

This afternoon I worked with Brother Brian, who had left the Oxford community in North Carolina and hoped to stay at the Genesee. We stored a load of timber in the attic of the laundry building. The wood was beautiful finished oak for the floor of the new church.

When I thought I had worked long enough, Anthony asked me to load heavy cement blocks in the pickup truck and unload them at a dumping place in the woods. I made two trips and then stopped. Anthony talked about the job as a small errand. After having made two trips— nearly causing a hernia—I told Anthony that I probably would be ready for the job by Christmas. He smiled.

During the day I often thought about a passage in *Zen and the Art of Motorcycle Maintenance* where Pirsig makes a distinction between ego climbing and selfless climbing. It seems a very important passage for me, worthwhile quoting here. Trying to explain why his eleven-year-old son, Chris, is not enjoying a camping trip to the ridge of a canyon, Pirsig writes: "To the untrained eye ego-climbing and selfless climbing may appear identical. Both kinds of climbers place one foot in front of the other. Both breathe in and out at the same rate. Both stop when tired. Both go forward when rested. But what a difference! The ego-climber is like an instrument that's out of adjustment. He puts his foot down an instant too soon or too late. He's likely to miss a beautiful passage of sunlight through the trees. He goes on when the sloppiness of his step shows he's tired. He rests at odd times. He looks up the trail trying to see what's ahead even when he knows what's ahead because he just looked a second before. He goes too fast or too slow for the conditions and when he talks his talk is forever about somewhere else, something else. He's here but he's not here. He rejects the here, is unhappy with it, wants to be farther up the trail but when he gets there will be just as unhappy because then the *it* will be 'here.' What he is looking for, what he wants, is all around him, but he doesn't want that because it *is* all around him. Every step's an effort both physically and spiritually because he imagines his goal to be external and distant."[1]

Pirsig seems to describe me and my problem. I came to the monastery to learn to live in the presence of God, to taste him here and now, but there is so much "ego-climbing" going on within me. I have so many ideas I want to write about, so many books I want to read, so many skills I want to learn—motorcycle maintenance is now one of them—and so many things I want to say to others now or later, that I do not SEE that God is all around me and that I am always trying to see what is ahead, overlooking him who is so close. From ego climbing to selfless climbing; that seems a good ideal for my retreat. But that is a long way and a high mountain.

Maybe I need to get stuck to learn it. I can't make selfless climbing an ego-trip! At another place in his book Pirsig writes: "Stuckness shouldn't be avoided. It's the psychic predecessor of all real understanding. An egoless acceptance of stuckness is the key to an understanding of all Quality, in mechanical work as in other endeavors."[2] This seems a very important thought. God help me when I get stuck. Until now everything has been so beautiful, so rich, so full of joy. I just want to say, "Thanks."

I'd better get some sleep now. Two o'clock is still a little early for me!

Friday, 7

Christian made a monastic outfit for me. He took me to the tailor shop, and we had some fun deciding how long the smock should be. I wanted it shorter than he, but we settled on the idea of "short and decent."

It feels good to wear a habit. Smock with attached hood, dark gray trousers, and a leather belt. Now I feel more a part of the community. I received quite a few smiles and remarks in sign language. People seemed to feel good about the "instant monk." This morning Christian put a note in my locker: "You appear excellent in the monastic habit and are doing very well fitting into the monastic life in general—best wishes for continued success." That is an encouraging note. Meanwhile, I feel a little bit like an overgrown dwarf from Snow White's court.

I have been reading the reports about the different abbeys. These reports were discussed in the general chapter in Rome last month. They tell about the life in the Trappist Communities around the world, summarize the problems, and give some suggestions. Since I know a few abbeys, I read the reports on them with special attention. While all eradiated a very sympathetic and overall positive tone, criticism was not avoided. Three aspects keep striking me: the crucial role of the abbot (much of the mood in a contemplative house seems to depend on his leadership); the struggle with poverty (some houses have become quite wealthy, and that remains a threat for the spiritual life); the problem of spiritual reading (spending "free time" well is not as easy as it seems, and the spiritual and intellectual formation needed for that is not always available). There seems to be an overall need for spiritual leadership.

During the afternoon I worked with Brother Brian in Salt Creek looking for granite stones for the new church. No easy task to differentiate between sandstones and granite stones since many stones are covered with lime which makes them all look alike at the start. But slowly I got a feel for it with the diagnostic help of the quiet Brian.

The whole afternoon I was struggling with the old question: Why didn't I really enjoy the work, and why did I want to go back to my books to read about the spiritual life? Is selecting stones in the creek bed not the best spiritual life possible? Why do I always want to read *about* the spiritual life and not really live it? Brian was so quiet and content, and I so restless and impatient. I kept saying to myself, "Just relax and enjoy what you are doing." After a while I felt better, found a few funny-looking stones, joked with Brian about finding gold (and closing the bakery!), and went home with a better feeling.

Saturday, 8

This morning I got my hands into the raisins. Brother Theodore, the "head baker," asked me to wash forty boxes of raisins. They had to be emptied on a sort of grill. Then the blocks of compressed raisins had to be broken up by hand and pushed gently through the grill. Theodore stood on the other end and checked to see if all was just raisins that came out. He obviously wanted to prevent people from having wood, paper, or stones in their bread.

During the last few days I have become good friends with Father John, one of the pioneering monks who came in 1951 from Gethsemani to lay the foundation of this monastery. Father John is a great lover of nature and a real expert on birds. This morning at 10 A.M. he took me out for what he called my "first lesson in birdwatching." It ended up being more of a lesson in bird hearing since we saw few birds but heard many. I was very impressed with the discerning ear of Father John. It must be a great joy to be able to walk through the woods recognizing all the sounds and having a dialogue with nature. I didn't even know the difference between chipmunk talk and bird talk. Well, I've a lot to learn about robins, warblers, orioles, and sparrows. Crows and the red-bellied woodpecker (who doesn't have a red belly but a red cap) were the easiest to recognize. But I also heard the catbird and the peewee. And when we walked home we saw a few chimney swifts playing high in the air. Meanwhile, I was bitten by mosquitoes.

The story of the bakery is worth telling. It all began with Brother Sylvester. Many years ago he started to use his navy experience by baking bread for the monks. He took his old navy recipe and changed it a little. He explained, "Since we were not allowed to eat butter on our bread, I tried to bake a kind of bread on which you don't need it. The guests who came to the monastery made so many good comments that I started to bake a few extra loaves." Well, soon orders started to come and the monks smelled not only bread but also business. Sylvester got his recipe patented. Some machinery was bought and soon "Monk's Bread" became a well-known specialty bread in upstate New York. Now three days a week around 15,000 loaves come off the conveyor belts. Sylvester works on the slicing machine and spends the rest of his working time as porter and shoemaker. At times he puts notes on the board such as this one: "I won't repair shoes any longer when the mud hasn't been taken off before they are brought to me!" Sylvester is a real monk and very humble. He also takes no nonsense.

I'd better start thinking a little more about my attitude toward work. If I have learned anything this week, it is that there is a contemplative way of working that is more important for me than praying, reading, or singing. Most people think that you go to the monastery to pray. Well, I prayed more this week than before but also discovered that I have not learned yet to make the work of my hands into a prayer.

Sunday, 9

After Lauds, John Eudes gave a talk about the Holy
Trinity. He was clear, succinct, mystical, and—extremely
practical. From the many things he said, what impressed
me most was the simple idea that the praise of God is the
criterion of the Benedictine life. He said, "Even the price
of our products and the use of our money should be determined by the praise of God's mysterious presence in our
lives." This hit me hard since I had just begun to realize
how much my own life was motivated by self-glory: even
going to a monastery could be a form of self-indulgence.
My problem with work is obviously related to my tendency to look at manual labor as a necessary job to earn a
couple of free hours to do my own work. Even when this
work seems very spiritual, such as reading about prayer, I
often look at it more as an opportunity to make interesting
notes for future lectures or books than as a way to praise
the Lord. I remember vividly how the Jesuits in high
school made me write above almost every page, A.M.D.G.
(*Ad Majorem Dei Gloriam*—To the Greater Glory of
God), but I am overwhelmed by the realization of how little of that has become true during the twenty-four years
since high school.

And still I know that living for the glory of God would
make everything different. Even living for each other
would then be living for the glory of God. It is God's
glory that becomes visible in a loving community. This
sounds pious and sweet but when John Eudes said, "We
get to know each other so well that we take each other for
granted and forget to realize that we are more than our
characters," I became aware of the powerful implications
of living for the glory of God. When we indeed participate in the life of God we will always discover more of
God's mystery in each other. John Eudes described
heaven as the ongoing discovery of God's mystery by liv-

ing in the most intimate presence of God and each other. The Christian life on earth is simply the beginning of this heavenly existence.

Monday, 10

This was a very good day, especially because I was not so preoccupied with "time for myself" and really enjoyed the work. While working on the bread-slicing machine, I said the Jesus Prayer—"Lord Jesus Christ, have mercy on me"—meditated on the question why people wanted to have their bread sliced instead of cutting it themselves, and learned a few technical things from Brother John Baptist about what to do when the bread gets cut the wrong way and a big mess comes out of the machine. I pushed the emergency button twice when the bread proved too high to fit in the plastic bag and started flying around. At least a beginning of insight.

Tuesday, 11

Today is the feast of the Apostle Barnabas. I never realized that the word Barnabas means "Son of Consolation." There was a beautiful hymn and also a reading from John Henry Newman about consolation during Vigils. Barnabas was described as a very gentle and caring man.

Nixon has gone on his trip to the Middle East. All the papers are writing about his attempts to distract attention from his Watergate problems. Nevertheless, impeachment seems to become more and more likely. I keep wondering about how I am responding to this. Shouldn't I pray for him and not just hope for sensational impeachment procedures? In many ways he is telling me about my own attachments and about the dangers of my own power games.

Thursday, 13

This afternoon I worked a few hours alone in the river carrying heavy granite rocks to the bank and making piles. While doing this, I realized how difficult "nepsis"—the control of thoughts—about which I read this morning, really is. My thoughts not only wandered in all directions, but started to brood on many negative feelings, feelings of hostility toward people who had not given me the attention I wanted, feelings of jealousy toward people who received more than I, feelings of self-pity in regard to people who had not written, and many feelings of regret and guilt toward people with whom I had strained relationships. While pulling and pushing with the crowbar, all these feelings kept pulling and pushing in me, and I often looked at the curve of the river, wondering if Brian would come to keep me company and help me to quiet them.

My reading about the spirituality of the desert has made me aware of the importance of "nepsis." Nepsis means mental sobriety, spiritual attention directed to God, watchfulness in keeping the bad thoughts away, and creating free space for prayer. While working with the rocks I repeated a few times the famous words of the old desert fathers: "fuge, tace, et quiesce" (live in solitude, silence, and inner peace), but only God knows how far I am, not only from this reality but even from this desire.

Once in a while I cursed when the rock was too heavy to carry or fell out of my arms into the water, making a big splash. I tried to convert my curse into a prayer: "Lord, send your angels to carry these stones," but nothing spectacular happened. I heard some red-winged blackbirds making some ugly noises in the air. My muscles felt strained, my legs tired. When I walked home I realized

that it was exactly the lack of spiritual attention that
caused the heaviness in my heart. How true it is that
sadness is often the result of our attachments to the world.

During dinner the reader, Brother Justin, started a new
book, *Or I'll Dress You in Mourning* by Larry Collins and
Dominique Lapiere. This is a book about the Spanish
bullfighter Manuel Benitez, "El Cordobez," who from a
poor Andalusian boy soon became one of the greatest
Spanish heroes of today. On the evening of his first
bullfight, he said to his sister who opposed his plans,
"Don't cry, Angelita. Tonight I'll buy you a house or I'll
dress you in mourning." Well, he bought more than a
house; he now owns hotels. I looked for a long time at his
picture in the book. The enormous tensions of his courageous bullfights have made his face heavy, serious, and
very sad. How will his life end? Will the people of Spain
allow him to die a non-heroic death? Since the beginning
of the bullfights in their present form (which was started
by Francisco Romero at the beginning of the eighteenth
century), more than four hundred torreros have been
killed by bull's horns. I am very curious to hear the whole
story. A vicarious way of watching a bullfight. What is it
in us that makes us so full of desires to see a man risk his
life? One answer is: Lack of nepsis.

Friday, 14

During the Eucharist this morning we sang: "Thus says
the Lord: By waiting and calm, you shall be saved. In
quiet and trust lies your strength" (Is. 30:15). That could
be the program for my restless soul for the coming six
months! I am impatient, restless, full of preoccupations,
and easily suspicious. Maybe I just need to repeat this
sentence very often and let it sink deep into my heart:
"By waiting and calm, you shall be saved. In quiet and
trust lies your strength." If these words could descend

from my head into my heart and become part of my innermost self, I would be a converted man. "Lord Jesus Christ, Son of the Living God, have mercy on me, a sinner."

For four and a half hours I worked with Brother Theodore and Brother Benedict at the raisin washer. Theodore washed, Benedict collected the raisins, and I folded empty boxes. Suddenly Theodore stopped the machine and knocked with his fist against his head. Not knowing sign language, I said, "What's the matter?" "A stone went through," he said. I asked him, "How do you know?" He said, "I heard it." I asked, "How could you hear it between the noise of the machine and the raisins cascading through it?" "I just hear it," he said, and added, "We have to find that stone. If a lady gets it in her bread, she can break her tooth on it and we can be sued!" Pointing to the large bathtublike container full of washed raisins, he said, "We have to push those through again until we find that stone."

I couldn't believe it. Benedict hadn't been able to detect the stone while the raisins came out, but Theodore was so sure that objection was senseless. Millions of raisins went through again, and just when I had given up ever finding that stone—it seemed like looking for a needle in a haystack—something clicked. "There it is," Theodore said. "It jumped against the metal wall of the washer." Benedict looked carefully and moved his hands through the last ounce of raisins. There it was! A small purple-blue stone, just as large as a raisin. Theodore took it and gave it to me with a big smile.

In some strange way this event meant a lot to me. Yesterday I was carrying granite rocks out of the river. Today we were looking for a small stone among millions of raisins. I was impressed, not only by Theodore's alertness, but even more by his determination to find it and take no risks. He really is a careful diagnostician. This little stone could have harmed someone—a lady or a monastery.

And I thought about purity and purification. Even the

small stone that looks like all these good-tasting raisins has
to be taken out. I can't even notice my own little sins, but
it offers me consolation to know that someone will keep a
careful watch on me and stop the machine when he hears
a stone between the raisins. That really is care.

Saturday, 15

Today I had my second talk with John Eudes. He invited me, and I was happy to have the opportunity to
have some time with him. I tried to express my feelings
about my first two weeks and to tell him not only that everything was well, but also that real inner silence and solitude were still far from my busy mind. He responded very
gently and recommended that I stay in my room more
even when I was just reading or studying. Until now I
had done all my reading and writing in the library where
people come and go. "Just try to be more alone—that will
help you to find solitude."

We also talked about work and the morbid creations of
the mind during routine actions in the bakery or in Salt
Creek. John Eudes said some very helpful things. "First of
all, it is certainly very hard not to have such thoughts.
Recognize them and let them pass. Secondly, keep doing
simple work that can attract your attention. It is good to be
interested in different types of rocks, in the songs of the
birds, in the varieties of trees, etc., but don't make a project out of it. Just enjoy it and be present to where you are
and what you are doing. And finally, try to find your own
rhythm. Ask yourself how much you can work without it
making you too tired to pray. It will take you a while to
find your balance."

Then we talked a bit about the hawks and foxes John
Eudes had seen and concluded with some discussions on
books. He thought that it was a good idea to read *The
Ladder of Divine Ascent* by John Climacus, which he
called "the most popular book in Eastern monasteries."

He also gave me a copy of his own translation of the *Praktikos* by Evagrius Ponticus, plus a *promanuscripto* copy of the *Apophtegms*, a collection of sayings attributed to the desert fathers.

I worked with Christian in the kitchen peeling potatoes. He has an ugly print of a sugar-sweet Madonna hanging above the stove. It would probably have made me think something less than friendly about Christian if he hadn't put in the frame of the same print a sign that reads in the most pompously decorated letters: BLESS THIS MESS. That only made me like Christian all the more. He has a sense of humor that puts all bad taste between parentheses.

Sunday, 16

Today is the feast of the Eucharist. After the Mass there was a short procession which included a simple ground-breaking ceremony for the new church. John Eudes put the blessed sacrament on a small altar near the front lawn, walked off with a big spade, turned some soil, said a few words about the new temple, and Anthony took a picture "for later generations." That was it.

What I want to talk about, however, is the conference John Eudes gave after Lauds. Because his meditations so obviously arise out of contemplation, John Eudes seems able to reach beyond the point where conservatives and progressives go different ways. He reaches a point so deep in the center of the spiritual life that he puts my suspicious spirit at ease and leads me away from the level where my mind tends to argue, agree, or disagree. I have always had some problems with feasts such as those of the Holy Trinity, the Blessed Sacrament, and the Sacred Heart. They seemed to arise out of a devotional period of the history of the Church in which I have a hard time feeling at home. It always seemed to me that the mystery of the Triune God, of the Divine presence in the Eucharist, and of the love of Christ for people are such central realities of the Christian life that you cannot set a special day aside to celebrate them. Certainly a special Sunday for the Eucharist never appealed to me. It was with this sort of rebellious mind that I went to listen to John Eudes. But what he said really took me away from these types of preoccupations and opened new horizons.

The Lord is at the center of all things and yet in such a quiet, unobtrusive, elusive way. He lives with us, even physically, but not in the same physical way that other elements are present to us. This transcendent physical presence is what characterizes the Eucharist. It is already the other world present in this one. In the celebration of the Eucharist we are given an enclave in our world of space and time. God in Christ is really here, and yet his physical presence is not characterized by the same limitations of space and time that we know.

The Eucharist can be seen only by those who already love the Lord and believe in his active, loving presence to us. But is that not true of every good relationship that we have? Friendship is like that, human love is like that. The bonds that unite us with those we love are invisible bonds. They become visible only indirectly, only by what we do as a result of them. But the bonds themselves are invisible. The presence of friends to one another is very real; this presence is palpably physical, sustaining us in difficult or joyful moments, and yet invisible.

Contemplative life is a human response to the fundamental fact that the central things in life, although spiritually perceptible, remain invisible in large measure and can very easily be overlooked by the inattentive, busy, distracted person that each of us can so readily become. The contemplative looks not so much around things but through them into their center. Through their center he discovers the world of spiritual beauty that is more real, has more density, more mass, more energy, and greater intensity than physical matter. In effect, the beauty of physical matter is a reflection of its inner content. Contemplation is a response to a world that is built in this fashion. That is why the Greek fathers, who were great contemplatives, are known as the dioretic fathers. *Diorao* means to see into, to see through. In celebrating the feast of Corpus Christi, the body of Christ, we celebrate the presence of the risen Christ among us, at the center of our lives, at the center of our very being, at the heart of our community, at the heart of the creation . . .

Monday, 17

When I woke up this morning I discovered that I was still in the habit of worrying about "what shall I do today —how shall I do it—what first, second, and third?" Then I realized that all this was no longer necessary. What I would do today would be decided by Brother Anthony, and the day would pass without worries about the order of things.

I think that most of my fatigue is related not to the type of work I do but to the false tensions I put into it. If I could just live the day quietly, obedient to the order of the day and the small instruction which I always find on a piece of paper stuck in my locker door (5:30–8:15, hot-bread line; 1–3, work with crew on lumber), then my mind would be more vacant for God and freer for the simple things of every moment.

I am beginning to discover the "other world" in which I live. When I run, monks smile; when I work very intensely, they make signs to slow down; and when I worry, I know it is usually useless. Last week I asked John Eudes how he thought that I was doing. He said, "I guess O.K. Nobody has mentioned you yet." That would not be a good sign everywhere! I really must enter that "other side," the quiet, rhythmic, solid side of life, the deep solid stream moving underneath the restless waves of my sea.

Some things are unexplainable. I guess the contemplative life is one of these things. Father Marcellus read a story about Beethoven during dinner. When Beethoven had played a new sonata for a friend, the friend asked him after the last note, "What does it mean?" Beethoven returned to the piano, played the whole sonata again and said, "That is what it means." This type of response seems the only possible response to the question, "What does the contemplative life mean?" Still you can keep writing about it just as people have been doing about Beethoven's works.

Today, David, twenty-three years old, entered the community as an "observer," and a long-haired, long-bearded, friendly young man from Brooklyn joined the family brothers. "I hope for life," he said. That sounded awesome to me.

Tuesday, 18

Sometimes when I think about my stay here with the Trappists, I think of myself as a cowbird. The cowbird is a lazy bird in so far as he does not build his own nest but lays his eggs in the nests of other birds—vireos, warblers, sparrows, and flycatchers. Some "hosts" are not very hospitable and puncture the stranger's eggs and throw them out. But most birds tolerate them. Well, I am not building my nest here but still want to lay my eggs in this Trappist place in the hope that they will tolerate them and give them their incubation time. I am very grateful for this hospitality and become more and more aware of how good people are to me. Yet I am not sure that I don't take this too much for granted, and I wonder what this "cowbird mentality" really means. Maybe there is a fear of real commitment. Maybe I keep acting too much as a parasite. It seems that God does not want me to become a Trappist. At least I discover very few indications in that direction. But it might be time to settle a little more solidly.

In the writings of the desert fathers there is much emphasis on renunciation and detachment. We have to renounce the world, detach ourselves from our possessions, family, friends, own will, and any form of self-content so that all our thoughts and feelings may become free for the Lord. I find this very hard to realize. I keep thinking about distracting things and wonder if I ever will be "empty for God." Yesterday and today the idea occurred to me that instead of *excluding* I could *include* all my thoughts, ideas, plans, projects, worries, and concerns and make them into prayer. Instead of directing my attention only to God, I might direct my attention to all my attachments and lead them into the all-embracing arms of God. When this idea grew in me, I experienced a new freedom and felt a great open space where I could invite all those I love and pray that God touch them with his love.

Meanwhile, nearly spontaneously, my Jesus Prayer changed from "Lord Jesus Christ, have mercy on me" into "Lord Jesus Christ, have mercy on us" and I felt as if all of creation could become transformed by the endless mercy of the Son of God.

Wednesday, 19

Since my greatest technical expertise until today has been driving a Volkswagen, Brother Anthony's order to drive the dump truck and transport huge loads of sand was quite a challenge. After asking casually for some help —"since I am not used to this type of truck"—I took to the road and worked my way through sandy corners to the great sand pile. If nobody knows how unpractical you are, they take it for granted that what you are doing is just routine. It went well. First, I thought that I had jammed up the second gear (of the six), but I was reassured by one of the brothers that "that strange noise is normal, just move fast to the third gear." Backing up was quite a problem since "mirror reading" is not my specialty. But I got to the right place and found the right levers and made the right moves to make the heavy load go "up and off." It still gives me the sensation of great power to operate those large machines, and I had the strange feeling of a well-spent afternoon. Just moving sand from one place to another—but the difference is between the shovel and the dump truck.

Thursday, 20

Tonight I had a dream about Thomas Merton. I never dreamed about him before, but this dream seems significant. I was with a small group of sisters sitting and talking in a recreation room in expectation of Thomas Merton, who was going to give a lecture. The atmosphere was casual and relaxed. The sisters were dressed in civilian clothes and were having a pleasant conversation.

Suddenly Merton appeared. He walked in with large steps. He was bald-headed and dressed in an all-white habit. Immediately after his appearance he left again, supposedly to get his notes for the talk. Then all the sisters vanished and returned within a few minutes all dressed in immaculate white robes. They sat down on the floor and took a very contemplative position. They did not say a word, looked very pious, and were obviously getting themselves ready to listen to the words of the great spiritual master.

When I left the room to see where Merton had gone, I found him in a small shed dressed in brown trousers, tennis shoes, and a yellow T-shirt with something written on it that I could not read. He was very busy fixing something. I started to help him, not knowing exactly how. I asked a few questions about nails and screws, but although he seemed very friendly, he didn't answer me. Then he started to clean an old yellow bench with sandpaper and repaint it with brown paint. I asked him where he got the sandpaper and the paint, but again he didn't answer while inviting me with a silent gesture to help him.

I was aware that the sisters were waiting for him to give the talk, but in some way it didn't seem to make sense to tell him this. I just started to paint with him. Then I woke up.

.The spiritual life does not consist of any special thoughts, ideas, or feelings but is contained in the most simple ordinary experiences of everyday living.

Friday, 21

Moods are worth attention. I am discovering during these first weeks in Genesee that I am subject to very different moods, often changing very quickly. Feelings of a depressive fatigue, of low self-esteem, of boredom, feelings also of anger, irritation, and direct hostility, and feelings of gratitude, joy, and excitement—they all can be there, sometimes even during one day.

I have the feeling that these quickly changing moods show how attached I really am to the many things given to me: a friendly gesture, pleasant work, a word of praise, a good book, etc. Little things can quickly change sadness into joy, disgust into contentment, and anger into understanding or compassion.

Somewhere during these weeks I read that sadness is the result of attachment. Detached people are not the easy victims of good or bad events in their surroundings and can experience a certain sense of equilibrium. I have the feeling that this is an important realization for me. When my manual work does not interest me, I become bored, then quickly irritated and sometimes even angry, telling myself that I am wasting my time. When I read a book that fascinates me, I become so involved that the time runs fast, people seem friendly, my stay here worthwhile, and everything one big happy event.

Of course, both "moods" are manifestations of false attachments and show how far I am from any healthy form of "indifference."

Thinking about all of this, I guess that my main problem still is that I have not really made prayer my priority. Still the only reason I am here—I mean, the only reason I *should* be here—is to learn to pray. But, in fact, much of what I am doing is motivated by many other concerns: getting back in shape, learning some manual skills, knowing more about birds and trees, getting to know interesting people—such as John Eudes—and picking up many ideas and experiences for future teaching. But if prayer were my only concern, all these other laudable things could be received as free gifts. Now, however, I am obsessed by these desires which are false, not in themselves, but by their being in the wrong place in the hierarchy of values. That, I guess, is the cause of my moodiness. For the time being it seems important to be at least aware of it.

Sunday, 23

John Eudes spoke this morning about "ardor." He remarked that although St. Benedict was always praised for his moderation, we should not overlook the ardor that permeates his Rule.

Ardor, fervent love, is especially brought to our attention during these days in which we celebrate the Sacred Heart of Jesus, the Immaculate Heart of Mary, and the feast of John the Baptist. Also Mary of Magdala and Mary of Bethany were both full of ardor in their penance and their love.

What struck me most in this conference was the idea that a fervent love was the basis for discernment. Neither John the Baptist nor St. Benedict was directly involved in the politics of his times. However, both were able to discern better from the periphery—the edge of the desert or

Monte Casino—the real ills of their times than those who were directly involved in organizing or reorganizing the social structures. Both might have been considered "provincial" in their days, but John the Baptist recognized the Lord, and St. Benedict, by his concentration on his own community, laid the foundations of a new Europe.

All these thoughts seem related to a short discussion I had with John Eudes yesterday about magazines and periodicals in the monastery. He felt that monks should be in touch with what goes on in the world, but felt that what he called "journalistic writing" is in conflict with the comtemplative vocation and makes the mind more dispersed than concentrated. For him that had meant the cancellation of the Abbey's subscription to *Commonweal* and the *New York Review of Books* and also the avoidance of the *National Catholic Reporter*, *Time*, *Newsweek*, and similar magazines.

I tend to agree with the principle but still feel very uncomfortable by the consequences drawn from it. In fact, the monastery ends up with quite conservative and even reactionary American clerical magazines. But John Eudes was open to suggestions. Meanwhile, I was happy to discover many excellent French and German periodicals.

During all this I became very much aware of the influence of the abbot on the minds of his monks. To be committed without becoming a fanatic and open-minded without becoming wishy-washy, is one of the main tasks of a contemporary abbot.

Monday, 24

This afternoon I had a long talk with John Eudes. He was very open, personal, warm, and made it easy to talk freely. I talked mostly about my anger: my inclination to become angry and irritated with people, ideas, or events. I had experienced angry feelings toward the easy decision to cancel subscriptions to "liberal magazines," toward feast days that had negative connotations, etc., etc. I realized that my anger created restlessness, brooding, inner disputes, and made prayer nearly impossible. But the most disturbing anger was the anger at myself for not responding properly, for not knowing how to express my disagreement, for external obedience while remaining rebellious from within, and for letting small and seemingly insignificant events have so much power over my emotional life. In summary: passive aggressive behavior.

We talked about this on many levels and in many ways. Most important for me at this point seem the following five suggestions:

First: Allow your angry feelings to come to your awareness and have a careful look at them. Don't deny or suppress them, but let them teach you.

Second: Do not hesitate to talk about angry feelings even when they are related to very small or seemingly insignificant issues. When you don't deal with anger on small issues, how will you ever be ready to deal with it in a real crisis?

Third: Your anger can have good reasons. Talk to me (John Eudes) about it. Maybe I made the wrong decision, maybe I have to change my mind. If I feel that your anger is unrealistic or disproportionate, then we can have a closer look at what made you respond so strongly.

Fourth: Part of the problem might be generalization. A disagreement with a decision, an idea, or event might make you angry at me, the community, the whole country, etc.

Fifth: On a deeper level you might wonder how much of your anger has to do with ego inflation. Anger often reveals how you feel and think about yourself and how important you have made your own ideas and insight. When God becomes again the center and when you can put yourself with all your weaknesses in front of him, you might be able to take some distance and allow your anger to ebb away and pray again.

These are some of the ideas I took with me from our meeting. John Eudes might have said them in this way or not. But in these words they remain with me. They give me enough to do.

We also talked about the history of the Abbey of the Genesee, about being an abbot, about some people we both know, and finally about the idea that solitude becomes really hard when you realize that nobody is thinking about you anymore. Then some place for God might become available in your occupied mind and heart.

It was a very good meeting. Gentle, open, warm, honest, and remarkably pleasant.

Wednesday, 26

While taking the hot loaves from the conveyor belt and trying to say the Jesus Prayer, my thought went to Spain and Angela Benitez, the mother of "El Cordobez," who died in Palma del Rio from hunger and exhaustion on May 7, 1941. From all I have read and heard during these weeks, the few pages about the death of this woman read during dinner settled most deeply in my mind.

This is how her daughter Angelita tells the story: "She kept looking at us, at each one of us standing around her. Manolo was so small then, his head hardly came up over the edge of the bed. He was crying, too, but he didn't know his mother was dying. My mother looked at me and cried. I don't think she suffered then but she was so worn from overwork and exhaustion, there was nothing left inside her. It was all used up. She slid her hand down the bed to where I was. She took my hand. There was no force in her hand anymore, that hand that had worked so hard. I had to hold it or it would fall. After a while she whispered to me, 'Angelita, Angelita, I give you your brothers and sisters. You will have to be their mother now.' A few minutes after that she was dead and all that was left of her was that tired look on her face. She was thirty-six."[3]

While taking the fresh hot loaves from the belt, I kept

seeing this woman in front of me. She would have been so happy with the hundreds of crumbs falling on the side and being swept away.

Her face became an accusation. When Angela died, I was nine years old. Manolo, her youngest son, now "El Cordobez," was five years old then. I was living in prosperity in Holland. He was on the edge of starvation a few hundred miles south of where I lived. And today? Do we have to wait until some African or Indian child becomes famous and worthy of a book to really feel and understand the suffering of his mother who is dying today?

Meanwhile, I realized how much I eat every day, much too much, and how hard it is to overcome my passion of gluttony, about which John Climacus and Evagrius wrote so eloquently. "Happy the poor"—I am wealthy, overfed, and well taken care of. The mother of Manuel Benitez was poor, really poor. I am eating bread without any limits. She had to eat grass, and today many are like her.

Do I have to go back to teach the well-dressed, well-sheltered, and well-fed? Are there other choices? What do I do with the money from writing books? "Angela Benitez, you will never be declared a saint, but to you I pray to help me become honest with myself."

Friday, 28

Anger is indeed one of the main obstacles of the spiritual life. Evagrius writes: "The state of prayer can be aptly described as a habitual state of imperturbable calm." The longer I am here, the more I sense how anger bars my way to God. Today I realized how, especially during work which I do not like much, my mind starts feeding upon hostile feelings. I experience negative feelings toward the one who gives the order, imagine that the people around me don't pay attention to my needs, and think that the work I am doing is not really necessary work but only there to give me something to do. The more my mind broods, the farther away from God and neighbor I move.

Being in a monastery like this helps me to see how the anger is really mine. In other situations there are often enough "good reasons" for being angry, for thinking that others are insensitive, egocentric, or harsh, and in those circumstances my mind easily finds anchor points for its hostility. But here! People couldn't be nicer, more gentle, more considerate. They really are very kind, compassionate people. That leaves little room for projection. In fact, none. It is not *he* or *they*, but it is simply *me*. I am the source of my own anger and no one else. I am here because I want to be here, and no one forces me to do anything I do not want to do. If I am angry and morose, I now have a perfect chance to look at its source, its deepest roots.

I always knew it: "Wherever you go, you always take yourself with you," but now I have nothing and no one to blame for my being me except myself. Maybe allowing this realization to exist is one little step on the way to purity of heart. How powerful are St. Paul's words: "Even if you are angry, you must not sin: never let the sun set on your anger or else you will give the devil a foothold. . . . Be friends with one another, and kind, forgiving each other as readily as God forgave you in Christ" (Ep. 4:26, 27, 32).

Tomorrow is the feast of St. Peter and St. Paul. Each a man of fervent temperament, both found their anger converted into an always-forgiving love.

Saturday, 29

Walking through one of the buildings where I hadn't been before, I came across a reproduction of Hazard Durfee's beautiful flute player with the text by Henry David Thoreau: "Why should we be in such desperate haste to succeed and in such desperate enterprises? If a man does not keep pace with his companions, perhaps it is because he hears a different drummer. Let him step to the music which he hears, however measured or far away."[4] It is quite understandable why one of the books on Thomas Merton is called *A Different Drummer,* and the longer I look at the quiet concentrated face of Durfee's flutist, the more I realize that the contemplative life is like hearing a different drummer.

Outside my window the song sparrow is singing loudly. For him it is not yet time to go to bed. It is seven o'clock and still very light. But I had better stop if I want to sing at 2 A.M. while the song sparrow sleeps.

Sunday, 30

This morning, during his weekly conference, John Eudes made a remark about the relationship between solitude and intimacy that touched me deeply. He said, "Without solitude there can be no real people. The more you discover what a person is, and experience what a human relationship requires in order to remain profound, fruitful, and a source of growth and development, the more you discover that you are alone—and that the measure of your solitude is the measure of your capacity for communion. The measure of your awareness of God's transcendent call to each person is the measure of your capacity for intimacy with others. If you do not realize that the persons to whom you are relating are each called to an eternal transcendent relationship that transcends everything else, how can you relate intimately to another at his center from your center?"

CHAPTER TWO

JULY

You Are the Glory of God

JULY

Monday, 1

At noon I had another session with John Eudes. I took up
the subject of my anger again and explained how often
my anger seemed related to experiences of rejection. I
mentioned three situations of the past week: a visitor to
the Abbey whom I know very well, but who didn't even
ask me how I was doing; students whom I had helped to
get summer jobs, but who didn't even drop me a note of
thanks; and a few monks who seemed unfriendly to me
without indicating any reasons. In all those cases I didn't
just feel a little irritated but felt deeply hurt, so much so
that in moments of prayer my thoughts became involved
in angry ruminations and revengeful scenes. Even my concentration during my reading got more difficult since practically all my energy went into the experience of the felt
rejection.

John Eudes pointed out my difficulties with "nuanced
responses." The problem, he said, is not that your feelings
are totally illegitimate. In fact, you might have a good
reason to feel rejected. But the problem is that your response has no proportion to the nature of the event. In
fact, the people you felt rejected by really don't mean that

much to you. But little rejections like these open up a huge chasm, and you plunge right into it all the way to the bottom. You feel totally rejected, unloved, left alone, and something like a "blind rage" starts developing that takes over and pulls you away from concerns and interests that are much more important to you. The problem is not that you respond with irritation but that you respond in a very primitive way: without nuances.

We tried to explore the reason for this fact. Somewhere there must be a need for a total affection, an unconditional love, an ultimate satisfaction. I keep hoping for a moment of full acceptance, a hope that I attach to very little events. Even something rather insignificant becomes an occasion for this full and total event, and a small rejection then easily leads to a devastating despair and a feeling of total failure. John Eudes made it very clear how vulnerable I am with such a need because practically nobody can offer me what I am looking for. Even if someone did offer me this unconditional, total, all-embracing love, I would not be able to accept it since it would force me into an infantile dependency which I, as an adult, cannot tolerate.

Why this need and the related fears? We both agree that right under the threshold of my "bravery," there is a tremendous insecurity and self-doubt that is easily triggered and laid bare by a small event. The great, often disproportionate, hostile sentiments are easily understood as reactions to a perceived threat to the core of my selfhood. We left it at that. It seemed quite a lot for forty-five minutes and certainly enough to think about for a week.

We also talked a little about Spain, Chile, and the Buddhists in South Vietnam.

Today we held a solidarity fast for the Buddhist monks who had refused to be enlisted in the army, had been put in jail, and had planned a hunger strike today. John Eudes and many others had sent protest telegrams. The result was a promise to release the monks. In fact, however, they were dispersed over many different prisons. At this moment nobody knew for certain if the fast was still being planned since the Buddhist monks were now separated from each other. No word had yet come about this from the Buddhist peace delegation in Paris. But we held a fast anyhow, and that certainly helped us to become more aware of the great suffering of other monks in this world.

Tuesday, 2

Today my friend Claude, who teaches political science, sent me some material on the Chilean crisis. The Chicago Commission Report and the Amnesty Report on the situation in Chile are so disturbing, so overwhelming in their description of the present terror, that I could hardly sleep last night. The description of the torture, the execution, and the all-pervasive oppression left me with a deep feeling of despair.

The Amnesty Report, summarized by Rose Styron in the *New York Review of Books*, makes it clear that we are not dealing here with a spasmodic explosion of revenge but with a well-organized system of oppression. Styron writes: "The sophistication and systematic use of methods of repression and revenge is the most depressing aspect of the current regime."[1] A note smuggled out of the Santiago stadium is one of the many witnesses. The author, a young man, writes: "They tied me to a table. They passed cables over my naked body. They wet me and began to apply currents to all parts of my body . . . blows began to my abdomen, ribs, chest, testicles. . . . They were laughing but assured me they were not kidding and threw acid on my toes. They stuck me with needles. . . . They took us back to the camp. There no one slept because of our moans. The prisoners cried with us. They took us another day and it was worse. . . . They did things that

cannot be told . . . threats of death if we didn't sign what
the interrogator wanted. 'No one knows about you,' he
said, and he tortured us. He was making fun of us. We
were no longer men. We were shadows. . . . This is our
ordeal. Why, my God, why? We trusted in justice" (Estado, Chile, February 1974).[2]

To realize that this goes on while I am sleeping quietly
in a monastery is very hard, and there is a tendency to
find a "mental solution" that gives sense to the contrast.
But nothing else than the naked absurdity of our human
condition came to my mind. The horrible thing is: It is
nothing new. It happened with the same systematic rigor
to the Jews under Hitler. I quote from the Chicago Commission Report: "The campaign of terror developed by
the Junta seems to have assumed a systematic and organized character. Repression is more selective than during
the first months following the takeover, but it is thorough
and well-prepared. Names of prisoners, their location and
details of arrest are computerized; it is assumed their lists
include potential prisoners as well."[3]

Occasionally during the last weeks I had problems with
the harshness of the psalms, but now they have become
easier to understand. When I identify myself with the
Chilean man who sent the note from the Estado, Chile, it
is not hard to say:

Let the groans of the prisoners come before you;
let your strong arm reprieve those condemned to die.
Pay back to our neighbors seven times over
the taunts with which they taunted you, O Lord (Ps. 78).

The proud have risen against me;
ruthless men seek my life:
to you they pay no heed.

But you, God of mercy and compassion,
slow to anger, O Lord,
abounding in love and truth,
turn and take pity on me . . .

Show me a sign of your favour
that my foes may see to their shame
that you console me and give me your help (Ps. 85).[4]

I could go on and quote many more psalms because after reading about Chile they become like burning prayers. I wish that those in prison could pray them and so find courage and strength.

When I let all the images of torture stories pass through my mind, I feel lost. What am I really experiencing? Powerlessness? Anger? Compassion? Restlessness? Desires to leave here and *do* something? Lack of faith in a loving God? Paralysis? It seems that all these feelings are there, all fighting for priority but constantly moving back and forth.

One question, however, seems important: Is it less compassion than just blind anger that dominates my emotions? When the torture scenes go through my head and I wonder what I would do, think, feel, or say in such a situation, I realize that there is a violent anger in me, a desire to see the torturers shamed, a hope for victory over those who do wrong. These feelings are really there and mostly stronger than feelings of compassion for those who suffer and of forgiveness for those who do them wrong.

Maybe it is realistic to recognize these feelings and be thankful that the psalms give me a chance to express them even in the intimacy of prayer. Maybe these feelings have to be led directly to the center of my relationship with my God, who is "slow to anger," and there converted into compassion and forgiveness. Maybe I am not ready yet to suffer for the Kingdom of God. My heart is too impure, my soul too divided, my love too fragile.

Before I fell asleep I wondered why I was here in the monastery. The one thing I am sure of is that I have to be here. There is a real *must*, but I honestly do not know what the purpose of it all is. When I think about Chile, I become very frightened.

This morning Anthony shaved my hair off. Practically

all of it. He started hesitantly to trim it a bit, but when I encouraged him to take off as much as he wanted, he went all the way and made my head as unsophisticated as that of all the other monks.

I must confess that I was attached to the little bit of long hair I had left, and when I looked at my shaved head in the mirror, I felt very strange. Somehow it seemed that someone had taken away something from me that I didn't want to let go, but somewhere I also felt that it was a good thing.

Hair cutting has many associations for me: Cardinal Alfrink cutting a little bit of my hair during the tonsure ceremony in Rijsenburg in 1955, Dutch women who collaborated during the war being shaved as punishment, Samson losing his hair and his strength, the rebellious hair of my friend Richard, the gentle long hair of Jim, Nancy, and Frank. But when I threw my hair in the waste basket, I thought that by cutting away individual difference—by becoming "one of us," as Anthony said—I might be more able to focus on the innermost personal uniqueness of my relationship with God and my fellow monks and come in closer touch with my real self.

Wednesday, 3

Today: feast of St. Thomas the Apostle. During a dialogue homily, two of the monks remarked in different ways that although Thomas did not believe in the resurrection of the Lord, he kept faithful to the community of the apostles. In that community the Lord appeared to him and strengthened his faith. I find this a very profound and consoling thought. In times of doubt or unbelief, the community can "carry you along," so to speak; it can even offer on your behalf what you yourself overlook, and can be the context in which you may recognize the Lord again.

John Eudes remarked that Dydimus, the name of

Thomas, means "twin," as the Gospel says, and that the fathers had commented that all of us are "two people," a doubting one and a believing one. We need the support and love of our brothers and sisters to prevent our doubting person from becoming dominant and destroying our capacity for belief.

Thursday, 4

A bad day. I felt low, depressed, morose, most of the day. The morning work in the bakery made me very tired. In the afternoon Anthony made me take down with a sledge hammer the part of the gatepost we couldn't finish last week. It was very hot and I just had no energy left. Meanwhile, I felt angry because with better equipment I could do in five minutes what would take me at least a day. I said this to Anthony, but he didn't change his mind and made a flippant remark about the monastic way of doing things. I then said that if monastic means impractical, I was not in favor of the monastic way. Well, a young fellow named Frank helped me a little, and Anthony brought a heavier sledge hammer. But I could hardly lift it.

Then Father Jean-Vianney, who was working close to me on the Trojan tractor shovel, saw me at work and said, "Relax, it is too hot for this—let me try to pull it out with the Trojan." He threw a heavy cable around the concrete post and attached it to the Trojan. He started the motor and pulled the whole post out of the ground as if it were a match. Well, I thanked him very much, cleaned the area, and went home.

My mind remained heavy, preoccupied with Brother Anthony's "monastic way of doing things" and my physical fatigue. I couldn't concentrate during Mass. For a moment I felt it would be better not to concelebrate in this mood, but I decided against it.

Meanwhile, I read that St. Dositheus became a saint

"because he had attached himself to obedience and had broken his own will."[5] Quite disconcerting reading in the context of a depressing day. I did not find much consolation in reading this. Somewhere there is an enormous gap to be bridged. I keep thinking, It is not only true that in order to become a saint you have to obey the will of God and detach yourself from your own will—but it is also true that you have to be a saint in order to allow your will to be interpreted by someone else as the will of God.

But this is a very hostile thought and lacks gentleness. I hope that tomorrow will be better.

Friday, 5

My depression lifted a little bit in the evening, mostly as the result of finding a room that was relatively cool, had good lights, and was far away from the noise of the carpenters and the truck drivers.

Saturday, 6

Today I read some valuable pages on spiritual direction in the "Instructions of Dorotheus of Gaza." He says: "Nothing is more harmful than self-direction, nothing more fatal. . . . I never allowed myself to follow my thought without asking advice."[6]

Collected many rocks with Father Stephen, Brian and John, a new observer. Sometimes our ambitions got out of hand and we tried to move unmovable rocks. There is a fine distinction between building a church and building a new tower of Babel. I think that there is a permanent temptation to forget the difference.

Sunday, 7

Today I read a short biography of Charles de Foucauld by Georges Gorree contained in a photographic essay on Foucauld's life.

I read this remarkable story again (after having read it in the seminary) in order to be able to think better about the desert fathers and their words in the context of our contemporary situation. I have to read more about this modern saint to understand fully what his life means to me. He left a wealthy life to become a hermit in the desert. Somewhere he wrote:

> Think————————
> that you must die as a martyr,
> robbed of everything,
> stretched out on the ground,
> naked, unrecognizable,
> covered with blood and wounds,
> violently and painfully killed—
> and desire
> that that may be today.[7]

On December 1, 1916, he was killed by a group of fellagah in Tamanrasset. Today I realized for the first time that Charles de Foucauld lived in two Trappist monasteries (in France and Syria) and, for a while, thought of becoming a Trappist monk.

Monday, 8

The most important part of this day was my meeting with John Eudes. I told him about my depression, my fatigue, my irritability, my frustrations of not having time to read, and my general feeling of exhaustion.

He responded very sympathetically. First of all, he explained that this was to be expected. He said that it took him a year to get used to rising at the early hour, and that manual labor, no meat, and other changes in life-style can, after the first enthusiasm has vanished, cause fatigue, depression, psychosomatic complaints, and questions about your vocation. When the monastic life does not hold anything new any more, when people do not pay any special attention to you any more, when nothing "interesting" is distracting you any more, then the monastic life becomes difficult. Then room opens up for prayer and ascesis.

Speaking about me, John Eudes felt that I should start by accepting my limitations and make small changes in my day for a while. After some discussion, it seemed best that on bakery days I should work only in the bakery and on the other days only during the morning or the afternoon. The extra time I should use for study. John Eudes felt that nothing should be forced, and that the first month of involvement had made me aware of my weaknesses and could now help me to rearrange my life. He also felt that I should not deny my desire to read and study more. "If you had plans to stay, living the ascetical life without much reflection might have been better, but for you it seems important that you have a chance to integrate your experience into your thinking more explicitly."

Then we talked awhile about the phenomenon that in the monastic setting you become so aware of very primitive needs. I told John Eudes that although I did not fast in any special way, I thought much more about food than ever before. He said, "We all want, desire, and need satisfaction, but in a context like this the traditional ways to get satisfaction—talking, attention, distractions, etc.—are not available. So you start responding more primitively; you start thinking about food and sex. You become much more aware of very basic cravings. In a sense, you fall apart, you regress, but it is also there that you become available for spiritual direction and can find a place for prayer and ascetical life. It is all a very sensitive thing. It can also lead to an egocentric preoccupation. You need guidance to prevent that."

It made much sense to me. It made me particularly aware of how much I was in need of guidance but also how grateful I should be to have a guide such as John Eudes at this point in my life.

Tuesday, 9

I saw a hummingbird this morning—a funny-looking little bird with a long bill with which it sucks nectar out of honey flowers. The hummingbird hums straight up, hangs in the air like a helicopter, and zooms away like a jet plane.

I am increasingly impressed by Dorotheus of Gaza. His chapter, "About resentment," could have been written by a very modern phenomenologist and was very good for me to read. It describes in detail how the mind can move from being troubled by a critical remark to being irritated, from irritation to anger, and from anger to vengefulness. Dorotheus quotes Evagrius Ponticus who says: "He who has conquered anger, has conquered demons. He, on the other hand, who is the victim of this passion, is an absolute stranger to the monastic life."[8] He describes in a vivid way how we can develop a morbid destructive inner attitude toward our neighbor. It might start with a little brooding about an ill-placed remark and grow into a devastating cancer that takes away our peace of mind, is harmful for the other, and leads us away from the road to God.

As the most important way to deal with this passion, Dorotheus points to prayer for him who has hurt us. Quoting Evagrius again: "He who prays for his enemies cannot be revengeful."[9]

The mother of Martin Luther King, Jr., was assassinated during a Sunday service in the Ebenezer Church in Atlanta. The assassin planned to kill her husband. I keep thinking about Martin Luther King, Sr., who has been the preacher in that church for forty years. God is really testing his faith. He lost his two sons and now his wife. You must be a saint to preach the Gospel after that with a pure heart, asking not for revenge but for forgiveness.

Wednesday, 10

Charles de Foucauld, the modern desert father, keeps me spellbound. Although his conversion to God after an obviously irreligious, pleasure-oriented youth, changed him profoundly, there is a remarkable sameness in this stubborn freedom during all the phases of his life. I am amazed how free this man was from peer pressure, how courageous in his disobedience, how persistent in pursuing a goal. With the same extremism that makes him defy military orders by taking his girl friend to Algiers and that makes him explore Morocco as an itinerant Jew, he gives himself to God.

In her book *The Sands of Tamanrasset*, Marion Mill Preminger creates a dialogue between Charles de Foucauld and his spiritual director, Abbé Huvelin, where this extremism becomes visible:

"Father," he said, "I should like to dedicate my life to God." Abbé Huvelin shook his head sadly: "You are not yet prepared, my son. You cannot yet be sure."

"From the moment I believed there was a God, I knew that I could not help living for him alone."

"You must not make such an important decision impulsively. You must think carefully."

"I have been thinking for two years, Father."

"You have been many things in your short life, my son. But when you leave the world to give yourself to God, there is no return."

"I have made up my mind, Monsieur l'Abbé."

Again the priest shook his head, "Prepare," he said. "Travel. Walk the sacred ground where Our Lord has walked. Pray where he has prayed. When you return, we will discuss your future."[10]

The sentence: "When you leave the world to give yourself to God, there is no return" hits me hard. It is an echo not only of Jesus' call to leave everything behind to follow him but also of the many voices of the desert fathers. I am more and more certain that I still have not left the world but keep lingering on the edges. I am plainly and simply scared of the "no return," and fear that the road of total commitment to God is arduous, painful, and very lonely. This reminds me of John Eudes' playful remark in Chapter: "We are not here on a sabbatical—for us, it is for keeps!" Everybody laughed and smiled kindly at me, but I realized that he had touched a central nerve of my spiritual life.

Trappist for life is something fundamentally different from Trappist for seven months. "Trappist for seven months," in fact, is a contradiction in terms. John Eudes said, "When I studied medicine and something happened that I didn't like, I could always say, 'Well, I will be out of this situation in a while.' When I was in the Navy and found the life disagreeable, I could always look forward to the day of my discharge, but when I was in the novitiate of the Trappists, there was not such a way out. This time it was 'for keeps,' and what was hard, unpleasant, or disagreeable had to be accepted and lived with as a way to purity of heart."

It is this type of extremism, of absolutism, of total surrender, of unconditional "yes," of unwavering obedience to God's will, that frightens me and makes me such a wishy-washy soul, wanting to keep a foot in both worlds. But that is how one stumbles.

Thursday, 11

Feast day of St. Benedict. I have been thinking how much I would like to be and remain close to this community of Benedictines. At this moment there is no sign that I should or could be a Trappist. Just as I am convinced that I should be here now, I am convinced that I should leave again. But could this become my community, my family, my "home," my point of orientation?

The Gospel today and John Eudes' sermon were telling the story. We are called to a radical break away from ourselves and a total surrender to God. St. Benedict, who so often is praised for his moderation and has even been called a humanist, is no less radical when he speaks about humility, obedience, and having everything in common.

If I wish to share in this radicalism, I should be willing to be fully obedient to my spiritual director; I should be humble enough to let him point the way; and I should be willing to share with him all my thoughts, feelings, and plans. Otherwise, the whole thing would be just romanticism.

I had many unexpected fantasies about my death today. I thought that this abbey would be the best place to be buried. But then I realized that a few months here hardly give one a title to be buried within the walls. John Eudes said in his sermon that most of the monks of this community had lived the rule of St. Benedict for more than half of their lives.

Friday, 12

When you keep going anxiously to the mailbox in the hope that someone "out there" has thought about you; when you keep wondering if and what your friends are thinking of you; when you keep having hidden desires to be a somewhat exceptional person in this community; when you keep having fantasies about guests mentioning your name; when you keep looking for special attention from the abbot or any one of the monks; when you keep hoping for more interesting work and more stimulating events—then you know that you haven't even started to create a little place for God in your heart.

When nobody writes anymore; when hardly anyone even thinks of you or wonders how you are doing; when you are just one of the brothers doing the same things as they are doing, not better or worse; when you have been forgotten by people—maybe then your heart and mind have become empty enough to give God a real chance to let his presence be known to you.

Saturday, 13

I have always had a strange desire to be different than other people. I probably do not differ in this desire from other people. Thinking about this desire and how it has functioned in my life, I am more and more aware of the way my life-style became part of our contemporary desire for "stardom." I wanted to say, write or do something "different" or "special" that would be noticed and talked about. For a person with a rich fantasy life, this is not too difficult and easily leads to the desired "success." You can teach in such a way that it differs enough from the traditional way to be noticed; you can write sentences, pages, and even books that are considered original and new; you can even preach the Gospel in such a way that people are made to believe that nobody had thought of that before. In all these situations you end up with applause because you did something sensational, because you were "different."

In recent years I have become increasingly aware of the dangerous possibility of making the Word of God sensational. Just as people can watch spellbound a circus artist tumbling through the air in a phosphorized costume, so they can listen to a preacher who uses the Word of God to draw attention to himself. But a sensational preacher stimulates the senses and leaves the spirit untouched. Instead of being the way to God, his "being different" gets in the way.

The monastic experience attacks this type of attention drawing. It asks you to say, write, and do things not differently but the same. It asks you to be obedient to age-long traditions and to form your mind and heart according to often proved and approved principles. In the spiritual literature I have read since I came here, there is a remarkable attempt to be faithful to the Gospel, to the words of the early fathers, to the insights of the spiritual director of the time, and an equally remarkable avoidance of trying to be different, sensational, and original. It seems that all the great spiritual writers are saying, "You cannot be original. If anything you say is worth saying, you will find its origin in the Word of God and his saints." What this place is calling me to be is—the same, and *more* of the same. The same as the monks, the same as the saints, the same as Jesus, the same as the heavenly Father. The rule of St. Benedict—the returning rhythm of the day, the continuous recitation of the 150 psalms and the uniformity of dress, food, and place—slowly makes you aware of a powerful sameness that transcends time and place and unifies you with the one God who is the Father of all people, all places, and all times, and who is the same through ages unending.

The monastic life is indeed very unsensational. I keep catching myself with the desire to do something special, to make a contribution, to add something new, and have to remind myself constantly that the less I am noticed, the less special attention I require, the less I am different, the more I am living the monastic life. Maybe—when you have become fully aware that you have nothing to say that has not already been said—maybe then a monk might be interested in listening to you. The mystery of God's love is that in this sameness we discover our uniqueness. That uniqueness has nothing to do with the "specialties" we have to offer that glitter like the artificial silver balls on a Christmas tree, but has everything to do with our most personal and most intimate relationship with God. When we have given up the desire to be different and experienced ourselves as sinners without any right to special attention, only then is there space to encounter our God who calls us by our own name and invites us into his intimacy.

Jesus, the only son of the Father, emptied himself "and being as we are, he was humbler yet, even to accepting death, death on a cross. But God raised him high and gave him the name which is above all other names" (Ph. 2:7–9). Only through ultimate sameness was Jesus given his unique name. When St. Paul calls us to have the mind of Jesus Christ, he invites us to that same humility through which we can become brothers of the Lord and sons of the heavenly Father.

Today was the feast of St. Henry. All the attention went to Brother Henry. I guess I had hoped for a little extra attention. Not getting it helped me to give a little more "flesh" to my meditation on sameness.

Painting was my afternoon job. The weather was beautiful—sunny and cool. I enjoyed scraping away the peeling paint, sandpapering and repainting the damaged spot, and looking out over the field from the vantage point where I was working. A big wasp kept me company the whole afternoon and did not sting. Brother Pascal said, "Don't make panicky moves. Just be gentle and it won't bother you." He proved to be right.

Sunday, 14

My father, who retired from the University of Nijmegen last year, wrote me: "As a man on pension, you see the world recede. No one needs you any more, so you have to stand on your own feet. Thus the Abbey will be a good preparation for that time which only seemingly is so far away from you."

My father is not a bitter man. The opposite: He is joyful, lively and full of energy. I even dare to say that he is more so since he has retired. Therefore, his words to me are very meaningful and very real.

I know too well how hard it is to live without being needed, being wanted, being asked, being known, being admired, being praised. Just a few years ago I retired from my teaching job in Holland and lived for a year as a student in a rented room in the city. I had expected to be free at last to study and do many of the things I couldn't do when I was so busy and so much in demand. But what happened? Without a job I was soon forgotten. People I had hoped would come and visit me didn't come; friends I expected to invite me remained silent; fellow priests whom I thought would ask me to assist them in their Sunday liturgy or to preach once in a while didn't need me; and my surroundings had pretty well responded as if I were no longer around. The irony was that I always wanted to be alone to work, but when I was finally left alone, I couldn't work and started to become morose, angry, sour, hateful, bitter, and complaining.

During that year I realized more than ever my vulnerability. That year of "quasi-retirement" showed me that being alone does not necessarily lead to inner peace and solitude of heart but can cause resentment and bitterness.

Now, three years later, I am back in the same situation. Every time I walk to the mailbox only to find it empty, some of the same feelings I had in Holland threaten to return. Even in this protective place with many good people around me, I am afraid of being forgotten, of being left alone. Yet I chose to be alone; I wanted it.

My father is very right when he says that the Abbey is a good preparation for the time when nobody will need me any longer. Here I have the chance to look at my emerging feelings of bitterness and hostility and unmask them as signs of spiritual immaturity. Here I have the chance both to be left alone and slowly to see this as an occasion to meet God, who will be faithful even when no one cares any longer. Here I have the chance to convert my feelings of loneliness into solitude and allow God to enter into the emptiness of my heart. Here I can experience a little bit of the desert and realize that it is not only a dry place where people die from thirst but also the vast empty space where the God of love reveals himself and offers his promise to those who are waiting in faithfulness. When I can open my heart just a little to my God, maybe I will be able to carry him with me into the world and to love my neighbor without becoming dependent on his gratitude or gifts.

Indeed, my retirement is only seemingly far away. Twenty-five years go fast, and who says that many forms of retirement will not be necessary much sooner? If, in a spiritual sense, I could retire now, that is, become independent of the success of my work, then I could probably live much more creatively and be much less vulnerable.

This monastic experience gives me some new understanding of what it means to "grow old gracefully," to live life less as an attempt to conquer new land and hold on to it and more as a grateful response to the gifts of God. In any case, this monastery is a good training place for aging.

Monday, 15

When I went to see John Eudes today my head seemed so filled with questions that I wondered how we could focus a little bit and bring some order into the chaos of concerns.

When I left I had the feeling that many things had indeed come together by focusing on the glory of God. The question, "How to live for the glory of God and not for your own glory?" has become very important to me. During the last weeks I have realized more and more that even my seemingly most spiritual activities can be pervaded with vainglory. There is something special and in some people's eyes "heroic" about going to the Trappists, and I wondered if it is really God I am seeking. Even my most intense attention to the ascetic and mystical writings of the early fathers easily turns into ideas and insights to be used for others' conversion instead of my own. Yes, there is a great temptation to make even God the object of my passion and to search for him not for his glory but for the glory that can be derived from smart manipulation of godly ideas.

John Eudes wasn't very surprised by my worries. He welcomed them as important enough to worry about, to think about, to live through.

How to dispel the passions that make us manipulate instead of worship? Well, the first thing to realize is that you *are* the glory of God. In Genesis you can read: "Yahweh God fashioned man of dust from the soil. Then he breathed into his nostrils a breath of life, and thus man became a living being" (Gen. 2:7). We live because we share God's breath, God's life, God's glory. The question is not so much, "How to live for the glory of God?" but, "How to live who we are, how to make true our deepest self?"

With a smile John Eudes said, "Take this as your koan:

'I am the glory of God.' Make that thought the center
your meditation so that it slowly becomes not only a
thought but a living reality. You are the place where God
chose to dwell, you are the *topos tou theou* (God's place)
and the spiritual life is nothing more or less than to allow
that space to exist where God can dwell, to create the
space where his glory can manifest itself. In your meditation you can ask yourself, 'Where is the glory of God? If
the glory of God is not there where I am, where else can
it be?'"

Obviously, all this is more than an insight, an idea, a
way of seeing things. That is why it is a subject for meditation and not so much for study. But once you start "realizing" in this very intimate and personal way that you
indeed are the glory of God, then everything is different,
then your life takes a decisive turn. Then, for instance,
your passions which seemed so real, more real than God,
show their illusory nature to you and sort of dwindle
away.

These thoughts led us to a short conversation about the
experience of God. I told John Eudes that for many years,
I had the fantasy that one day God just might break
through the hard shell of my resistance and reveal himself
to me in such an intensive and convincing way that I
finally would be able to let my "idols" go and commit myself unconditionally to him. John Eudes, not too surprised
by the fantasy, said, "You want God to appear to you in
the way your passions desire, but these passions make you
blind to his presence now. Focus on the nonpassionate
part of yourself and realize God's presence there. Let that
part grow in you and make your decisions from there. You
will be surprised to see how powers that seem invincible
shrivel away."

We talked about many more things, but what I remember best of the final part of our conversation was the
idea that I should be happy to be part of the battle, independent of the question of victory. The battle is real, dangerous, and very crucial. You risk all you have; it is like
fighting a bull in a bull ring. You will only know what vic-

tory is when you have been part of the battle. People who have tasted real victory are always very modest about it because they have seen the other side and know that there is little to brag about. The powers of darkness and the powers of light are too close to each other to offer the occasion for vainglory. That's what a monastery is all about. In the many little things of everyday life we can recognize the battle. It can be as small as a desire for a letter or a craving for a glass of milk. By staying at one place you get to know the battlefield quite well.

Tuesday, 16

I had the following thought: At the moment that I have a strong and real desire to stay here for life, I am ready to leave. Because at the moment that I feel the inner readiness to live my life only for the glory of God, I am ready to live creatively in the world and be open to my neighbors, since then I no longer depend on their affection.

Dorotheus writes: "Don't look for the affection of your neighbor. He who looks for it is troubled when he does not get it. You yourself, however, have to give witness to the love for your neighbor and to offer him rest, and thus you will bring your neighbor to love."[11]

Wednesday, 17

One of the things a monastery like this does for you is give you a new rhythm, a sacred rhythm. While teaching in New Haven I was very much aware of Sunday as a special day, but beyond that all the days seemed the same —only different in their relationship to the school calendar. Here the rhythm is different. Not only Sundays are different, but all the days of the week have their own nuance, determined by the psalms and hymns you sing,

the Scripture lessons you hear, and, most of all,
Eucharist you celebrate. In the beginning I was
aware of how I was being pulled slowly into a ne\.
style, a new way of perceiving time and a new way of experiencing God's presence. But now after more than a
month of participating in the daily rhythm of this community with a minimum contact with my previous life, I find
myself thinking about the Holy Trinity, the life of Christ,
about St. John the Baptist, St. Benedict, St. Bonaventure,
about an often repeated Gospel passage, a certain psalm,
and a catch phrase in a biography of a saint. It seems as if
I am being slowly lifted up from the gray, dull, somewhat
monotonous, secular time cycle into a very colorful, rich
sequence of events in which solemnity and playfulness,
joy and grief, seriousness and lightness take each other's
place off and on.

It is an important experience for me to celebrate the
feast days of the saints again. In the milieu in which I
have worked the last three years, there is hardly any room
for saints, but here saints are like roommates with whom
you can have long conversations. Sometimes I can't keep
up with the feasts of saints. One day the whole house
seems filled with praise to God because of St. Benedict,
but when I just have started to read his life, everyone else
is already excited about another saint. Moreover, since the
monks celebrate not their birthdays but their saint's days,
many feast days have special meaning for individual
monks. That gives it all an even more personal touch.

I remember from my high school years with the Jesuits
and from my seminary years, how the secular and the sacred cycles always intersected each other. But here there
is nothing to intersect with. Here the only cycle is the liturgical cycle, and here the time is indeed redeemed. You
see and feel that the monastic day, week and year are
meant to be time-bound anticipations of a heavenly existence. Already you are invited to participate in the intimate life of the Holy Trinity, Father, Son, and Spirit, and
to be joyful because of those who came so close to God in
their historical existence that they have a special place in

the heavenly kingdom. So contemplation is indeed a beginning of what is to be fulfilled in the resurrection.

Today was the feast day of my neighbor in choir, Brother Alexis. He looked happy and radiant.

Thursday, 18

I hardly remember what it was, but a small critical remark and a few irritations during my work in the bakery were enough to tumble me head-over-heels into a deep, morose mood. Many hostile feelings were triggered and in a long sequence of morbid associations, I felt worse and worse about myself, my past, my work, and all the people who came to mind. But happily I saw myself tumbling and was amazed how little was needed to lose my peace of mind and to pull my whole world out of perspective. Oh, how vulnerable I am!

The milieu of this place full of prayerful people prevents me from acting out, from getting angry, from bursting open. I can sit down and see how quickly the little empty place of peace in my heart is filled again with rocks and garbage falling down from all sides.

It is hard to pray in such a mood. But still during Terce, the short prayer immediately after work, standing outside in our dirty work clothes, we read: "Is anyone among you in trouble? He should turn to prayer." Indeed prayer is the only real way to clean my heart and to create new space. I am discovering how important that inner space is. When it is there it seems that I can receive many concerns of others in it without becoming depressed. When I sense that inner quiet place, I can pray for many others and feel a very intimate relationship with them. There even seems to be room for the thousands of suffering people in prisons and in the deserts of North Africa. Sometimes I feel as if my heart expands from my parents traveling in Indonesia to my friends in Los Angeles and from the Chilean prisons to the parishes in Brooklyn.

Now I know that it is not I who pray but the spirit of God who prays in me. Indeed, when God's glory dwells in me, there is nothing too far away, nothing too painful, nothing too strange or too familiar that it cannot contain and renew by its touch. Every time I recognize the glory of God in me and give it space to manifest itself to me, all that is human can be brought there and nothing will be the same again. Once in a while I just know it: Of course, God hears my prayer. He himself prays in me and touches the whole world with his love right here and now. At those moments all questions about "the social relevance of prayer, etc." seem dull and very unintelligent, and the silent prayer of the monks one of the few things that keeps some sanity in this world.

But then again, how little it takes to have everything cave in on me and make my heart into a dark place of ignorance! Just today I read: "Faith is a thought of God free from passion."[12] How meaningful that sounds after a passionate day.

Friday, 19

During the four and a half hours of raisin washing this morning, I couldn't concentrate on anything except the desire to see the last raisin go through the machine.

In U. S. News and World Report, I read that Edwin Aldrin, the second man on the moon, wrote a book, Return to Earth, describing his problems of adjusting to a world in which he finds no more goals to reach. It also says that he is afflicted by moments of deep depression. I would like to understand his depression better. Having visited the moon must have affected his understanding of the earth profoundly.

Saturday, 20

Reflecting on my past three years of work, I realize more and more that it lacked unity. The many things I did during those years seem disjointed, not really relating to each other, not coming from one source. I prayed during certain hours or days but my prayer seemed separated from the lectures I gave, the trips I made, the counseling I did. When I think of the many lecture invitations I declined with the argument that I had no time to prepare, I see now how I looked at every speaking engagement—be it a lecture, a sermon or a commencement address—as a new performance that calls for new preparation. As if I had to entertain a demanding audience that could not tolerate any poor performance. No wonder that this attitude leads to fatigue and eventually to exhaustion. Even small daily tasks such as talking with your own students becomes an anxiety-provoking burden.

Now I see that I was all mixed up, that I had fragmented my life into many sections that did not really form a unity. The question is not, "Do I have time to prepare?" but, "Do I live in a state of preparedness?" When God is my only concern, when God is the center of my interest, when all my prayers, my reading, my studying, my speaking, and writing serve only to know God better and to make him known better, then there is no basis for anxiety or stage fright. Then I can live in such a state of preparedness and trust that speaking from the heart is also speaking to the heart. My fears and my resulting fatigue over the last three years might well be diagnosed as a lack of single-mindedness, as a lack of one-eyedness, as a lack of simplicity. Indeed, how divided my heart has been and still is! I want to love God, but also to make a career. I want to be a good Christian, but also have my successes as a teacher, preacher, or speaker. I want to be a saint, but also enjoy the sensations of the sinner. I want to be

close to Christ but also popular and liked by many people.
No wonder that living becomes a tiring enterprise. The
characteristic of a saint is, to borrow Kierkegaard's words,
"To will one thing." Well, I will more than one thing, am
double-hearted, double-minded, and have a very divided
loyalty.

"Set your hearts on his kingdom first . . . and all these
other things will be given you as well" (Mt. 6:33). Jesus
is very clear about it. You cannot love God and mammon,
you cannot be for him and against him, you cannot follow
him just a little bit. Everything or nothing.

John Eudes said that his conferences with the monks
grew out of his meditations. They were like sharing with
others his own prayer. If I could slowly come to that trust
in God, that surrender, that childlike openness, many tensions, and worries would fall away, would be unmasked
as false, empty, unnecessary worries, not worth the time
and energy, and I could live a simple life. My preaching
and teaching, my lecturing and counseling could be like
different forms of a meditative life. Then I probably
would have an open mind, open to perceive many things I
didn't notice before, open to hear many people I didn't
hear before. Then I wouldn't worry about my name, my
career, my success, my popularity and would be open to
the voice of God and his people. Then I probably also
would know much better what is worth doing and what is
not, which lectures to accept and which to refuse, which
people to spend time with and which people to keep at a
distance. Then I most likely would be less plagued by passions causing me to read the wrong books, hang around
the wrong places, and waste my time with the wrong
company. Then—no doubt—I would have much more time
to pray, to read, to study, and to be always prepared to
speak the word of God when the right time has come.
Wherever I am, at home, in a hotel, in a train, plane, or
airport, I would not feel irritated, restless, and desirous of
being somewhere else or doing something else. I would
know that here and now is what counts and is important

because it is God himself who wants me at this time in this place.

Here in the safe surrounding of the Abbey I can see it all quite clearly. I hope that some of that vision will last when I leave this place and enter again the fragmented and fragmenting world.

One of the monks said to me today, "Monks are like children: very shy and very sensitive. When you ruffle them, they tend to withdraw. They are not like college students who can take some mental pushing and pulling. They are very vulnerable, and if you come on too strong, they might respond by hiding themselves from you."

Sunday, 21

On Sundays there always is a bouquet of flowers in front of the altar. Today it was a bouquet of wheat to announce the wheat harvest which is to start tomorrow. The sight moved me deeply. Not just because of the obvious relationship between the wheat and the mystery of the Eucharist, but also because of our growing knowledge of the lack of wheat in the northern countries of Africa.

A letter from the White Fathers who have their missions in Africa was on the bulletin board. A despairing letter telling about the starvation of millions of people while we in the U.S.A. publish articles about how to reduce weight. During the Roman Empire these same African countries were prosperous, full of wheat and cattle. Now they are a desolate desert growing wider and wider. In Chapter, John Eudes spoke about his visit to Nigeria in May. He told how the farmers kept plowing their dry land simply so that they might not lose their skill but without hope of a harvest. Every year the desert advances from three to twenty miles. Every year fewer miles to cultivate and more miles of dry, fruitless sand.

And we? John Eudes said, "When I returned from

Africa, our land looked like paradise—green, rich, fruitful."
What is it that makes us able to produce so much and unable to share it with starving people only eighteen flight hours away?

It is a number of complex factors. But whatever the explanations are, they cannot keep us from feeling that we haven't done enough to prevent it. Brother Anthony asked, "Do we know where *our* wheat is going?" The answer was, "Only that it will be eaten by people and not by animals, but by whom it is eaten is beyond our control."

It is necessary to think more about all this and to act wisely. When I think about my work after I leave this monastery, I must ask myself how it relates to this world problem, which unquestionably will be with us for many years to come. For now, it seems that some fasting is the best way to remind myself of the millions who are hungry and to purify my heart and mind for a decision that does not exclude them.

Monday, 22

Today during my meeting with John Eudes I discussed my relationship to Our Lady, the Blessed Mother of God. When I was a child she played a very important role in my religious development. The May and October devotions in my family are a real part of my childhood memories. We built little altars, sang songs, prayed rosaries, and seemed to enjoy it. But after my seminary years, a certain antidevotionalism developed in the circles where I lived, and Mary, the Mother of Jesus, became less and less important in my religious life.

But this week "she returned." Not by any conscious attempt to restore my devotion to Our Lady or by a book or any advice, but without any intrusiveness I found her in the heart of my search for a more contemplative life. If anything helped, it was the Icon of Our Lady of Vladimir

in the Abbey chapel. I couldn't keep my eyes off this most
gentle painting which, in fact, is a reproduction made by
a monk of Gethsemani.

With a somewhat sad, melancholic gaze, Mary looks at
you and points with her right hand to the child she holds
on her left arm. The child is embracing her in a very
affectionate way. The intimacy of the child's embrace is
expressed by the little hand that, appearing from under
the veil covering Mary's head, gently touches her left
cheek. The child looks like a small adult in a monk's habit.

I keep looking at this intimate scene, and peace invades
my soul. Mary speaks to me about Jesus. To him she directs me but without fearful warnings, without strong
challenges, without a demanding stern look. It is as if she
says, "Look, he who is your Lord and Salvation has become small and vulnerable for you. Why don't you come
closer and listen to what he has to say?" At the same time
it seems that she invites me to share in the intimacy between her and her child.

This week I often experienced resistance toward private
prayer. Every time I tried to sit down and pray alone my
thoughts wandered to the book I was reading and wanted
to continue reading, to my feelings of hunger, to a monk I
couldn't figure out, to a hostile feeling or a daydream I
couldn't shake off. Usually I ended up reading a few minutes trying to focus my thoughts again. But when I knelt
in front of the Icon of Our Lady of Vladimir, it was
different. In some way my resistance against meditation
subsided, and I simply enjoyed being invited to enter into
the intimacy between Jesus and Mary.

John Eudes didn't run away from the psychological implications of all this. He made me see how masculine my
emotional life really is, how competition and rivalry are
central in my inner life, and how underdeveloped my feminine side had remained. He told me about St. Bernard,
who didn't hesitate to call the task of the monk a woman's
task (compared with the virile task of the secular priest)
and to remind the abbot (the word comes from ab-
ba=father) of his motherly responsibilities. John Eudes

also reminded me that the Hebrew word for God's Spirit, *Ruach*, is both masculine and feminine, and thus emphasizes that God is male and female. Mary helps me to come in touch again with my receptive, contemplative side and to counterbalance my one-sided aggressive, hostile, domineering, competitive side. "It is not so surprising that you are easily depressed and tired," he said. "Much of your energy is invested in keeping your hostilities and aggressions under control and in working on your appearance of gentleness and kindness."

I hope and pray that through a renewed devotion to Our Lady, the Blessed Mother of God, I can allow my other side to grow to maturity and to become less self-conscious, less suspicious, less angry, and more able to receive God's gift, more able to become a contemplative, more able to let the Glory of God dwell in me as it dwelled so intimately in Mary.

Tuesday, 23

In the contemplative life every conflict, inner or outer, small or large, can be seen as the tip of an iceberg, the expressive part of something deeper and larger. It is worthwhile, even necessary, to explore that which is underneath the surface of our daily actions, thoughts, and feelings.

The most persistent advice of John Eudes in his spiritual direction is to explore the wounds, to pay attention to the feelings, which are often embarrassing and shameful, and follow them to their roots. He keeps telling me not to push away disturbing daydreams or hostile meanderings of the mind but to allow them to exist and explore them with care. Do not panic, do not start running but take a careful look.

It is interesting to mention here Diadochus of Photice's views on the discernment of spirits. He says that we have to keep the surface calm so that we can see deep into the soul. "When the sea is calm, the eyes of the fishermen can penetrate to the point where he can distinguish different movements in the depth of the water, so that hardly any of the creatures who move through the pathways of the sea escape him, but when the sea is agitated by the wind, she hides in her dark restlessness what she shows in the smile of a clear day."[13]

What is the importance of this? Diadochus says that with a clear mind we will be able to distinguish the good from the bad suggestions so that the good ones can be treasured and the bad ones dispelled.

That indeed is the value of being able to follow the movements of the soul. When we do not panic and create waves, we will be able to "think them through" to the end. When the end proves to be a dead end, a blind alley, then we can be free to search for a new way without the false suspicion that the old way might be the better one. When we keep a diagnostic eye on our soul, then we can become familiar with the different, often complex stirrings of our inner life and travel with confidence on the paths that lead to the light.

I was surprised and happy to find a somewhat similar idea in the sermon of Bernard of Clairvaux to the university students in Paris. There he says: ". . . he who hears the word of the Lord: Return ye transgressors to the heart (Is. 46:8) having discovered such great obscenities in his inmost self, like some eager explorer makes every effort to trace them to their sources one by one and to learn how it was that they entered there."[14] Bernard shows how a radical understanding of our evil thoughts leads to a confession of our sinfulness and sets us free to accept God's compassion and mercy: "that weakness which is serviceable is the weakness which seeks the aid of a physician."[15]

These many images and ideas might sound somewhat confusing but two ideas are clear. First: Do not run away from your inner feelings even when they seem fearful. By following them through you will understand them better and be more free to look for new ways when the old ways run into a blank wall. Second: When you explore in depth

your unruly and wild emotions you will be confronted
with your sinful self. This confrontation should not lead to
despair but should set you free to receive the compassion
of God without whom no healing is possible.

Today I collected rocks with Brian while the rain
poured down on us. When we came home, we looked like
two drowned cats, but everyone is grateful for the rain
after three dry weeks. It interrupts the wheat harvest, but
the wheat will be better for it.

Wednesday, 24

I would like to think a little more about love. This monastery definitely exudes a real atmosphere of love. You can
indeed say, the monks love each other. I even dare to say
they show a real love to me. I think that this is a very important experience because they not only make me feel
love but also help me to understand love better.

My first inclination has been, and in many ways still is,
to connect love with something special in me that makes
me lovable. When people are kind and friendly toward
me, I feel happy because I think that they are attracted to
me and like me in a special way. This more or less unconscious attitude got me into trouble here since the monk
who is nice and good to me proves to be just as nice and
good to everyone else. So it becomes hard to believe that
he loves me because of something special that I have and
others do not have. I am obviously not more or less attractive than others. This experience was in the beginning a
painful one. I tended to react by thinking, "Well, if he is
just as friendly to everyone else as he is to me, his friendliness cannot be real. It is just one of those poses, one of
those 'frozen smiles.' He is friendly because he is supposed
to be friendly. He is just following the rule. His love is
only the result of obedience. It is not natural, not sponta-

neous, not real. Underneath his friendly surface he probably couldn't care less about me as an individual."

But these ruminations were exactly that: ruminations. I
knew that I was fooling myself, that there was something
very important I was missing. I knew it simply because
the story I told myself was not true. The monks who show
me love, show love to me not as an abstraction but as a
real individual with his own strengths and weaknesses,
habits and customs, pleasant and unpleasant sides. The
love they show me is very alert, awake, and based on the
real me. When I ask something, they listen with attention
and try to help me, and when I show a need for support,
information, or interest, they offer me as well as they can
what I need. So although their love for me is not exclusive, particular, or unique, it is certainly not general, abstract, impersonal, or just an act of obedience to the rule.

It is important for me to realize how limited, imperfect,
and weak my understanding of love has been. Not my
theoretical understanding but my understanding as it reveals itself in my emotional responses to concrete situations. My idea of love proves to be exclusive: "You only
love me truly if you love others less"; possessive: "If you
really love me, I want you to pay special attention to me";
and manipulative: "When you love me, you will do extra
things for me." Well, this idea of love easily leads to van-
ity: "You must see something very special in me"; to jealousy: "Why are you now suddenly so interested in someone else and not in me?" and to anger: "I am going to let
you know that you have let me down and rejected me."

But love is "always patient and kind; it is never jealous;
love is never boastful or conceited; it is never rude or
selfish; it does not take offense, and is not resentful" (I
Cor. 13:4–5).

It is this understanding of love that I must slowly learn.
But how? It seems that the monks know the answer, "You
must love the Lord your God with all your heart, with all
your soul, with all your mind." This is the greatest and the
first commandment. It seems that the life the monks are
living is a witness to the importance of keeping the first

commandment first so that the second, "which resembles it" can be realized as well: "You must love your neighbor as yourself" (Mt. 22:37–39). I am beginning to experience that an unconditional, total love of God makes a very articulate, alert, and attentive love for the neighbor possible. What I often call "love for neighbor" too often proves to be a tentative, partial, or momentary attraction, which usually is very unstable and does not last long. But when the love of God is indeed my first concern, a deep love for my neighbor can grow.

Two more considerations may clarify this. First of all, I discover *myself* in a new way in the love of God. St. Bernard of Clairvaux describes as the highest degree of love the love of ourselves for God's sake. Thomas Merton commenting on this says: "This is the high point of Bernard's Christian humanism. It shows that the fulfillment of our destiny is not merely to be lost in God, as the traditional figures of speech would have it, like a 'drop of water in a barrel of wine or like iron in the fire' but found in God in all our individual and personal reality, tasting our eternal happiness not only in the fact that we have attained to the possession of his infinite goodness, but above all in the fact that we see his will done in us."[16]

Secondly, it is not only ourselves we discover in our individuality but our fellow human beings as well, because it is God's glory itself that manifests itself in his people in an abundant variety of forms and styles. The uniqueness of our neighbors is not related to those idiosyncratic qualities that only they and nobody else have, but it is related to the fact that God's eternal beauty and love become visible in these unique, irreplaceable, finite human beings. It is exactly in the preciousness of the individual person that the eternal love of God is refracted and becomes the basis of a community of love.

When we have found our own uniqueness in the love of God and have been able to affirm that indeed we are lovable since it is God's love that dwells in us, then we can reach out to others in whom we discover a new and unique manifestation of the same love and enter into an intimate communion with them.

The guestmaster, Father Francis, showed me a letter of gratitude written by the leader of a group of retarded boys who visited the monastery last week. It is a moving letter. Vespers had impressed them the most. One boy, who was used to being elbowed out of church because of his "litany of obscenities," was surprised that this did not happen this time and asked to go back again.

Indeed, I think that often those who are poor at verbal communication sense better the mood and atmosphere of a place or an event than very cerebral, "discussing" types. These retarded boys had sensed the mystery hidden under the meanings of the words.

Friday, 26

Since I have lived in this Abbey of the Genesee, I have written many more letters than I planned to write when I came. My original idea was: no telephone, no letters, neither outgoing nor incoming, no visitors, no contact with guests—but a real retreat "alone with the Alone."

Well, most of my plans are coming through except for my letter writing. Is this good or an initial sign of compromise? Maybe both.

One of the experiences of silence is that many people, good old friends and good old enemies, start seeking attention. Often a thought led to a prayer and a prayer to a letter and a letter to a real feeling of peace and warmth. A few times, after having dropped a small pile of letters in the mailbox, I had a deep sense of joy, of reconciliation, of friendship. When I was able to express gratitude to those who had given me much, sorrow to those whom I had offended, recognition to those I had forgotten, or sympathy to those who are in grief, my heart seemed to grow and a weight fell from me. These letters seemed to restore the part of me wounded by past resentment and take away the obstacles that prevented me from bringing my history into my present prayer.

But there also is another side. Perhaps part of my letter writing shows that I do not want to be forgotten here, that I hope that there still are people "out there" who think of me. Maybe part of my letter writing is my newly found way of seducing people into paying attention to me here in the enclosure of a monastery. I am sure that that is part of it because just as I feel happy when I drop my letters in the mailbox, so do I feel disappointed when I don't receive much in return. Then my heroic remarks about not writing to my friends shrivel into feelings of being forgotten and left alone.

I thought about all of this when I read about the remarkable friendship between Bernard of Clairvaux and William of St. Thierry, both very sensitive people but very different characters. William, Abbot of a Benedictine Monastery, had a great admiration and affection for Bernard. He wrote him many letters, but Bernard did not always respond as fast as William hoped he would. Once after many unanswered letters, William wrote: *"Plus amans, minus diligor."* (I love more than I am loved.) This was enough to provoke Bernard to a long passionate answer: "You can reach me if you but considered what I am, and you can reach me still whenever you wish if you are content to find me as I am and not as you wish me to be." In this and many other sentences Bernard responded to the suggestion that his affection for William was less than William's for him.

Louis Bouyer, discussing this exchange, remarks dryly: ". . . it remains no less clear that what was happening with Bernard was what so often happens with very sensitive and passionate people. So long as he had his friends in mind, he was entirely taken up with the thought of them; but he could very well go for a month without thinking of them."[17]

There is much of William of St. Thierry's need for friendship in me, and sometimes that need shows more a lack of a real sense of self than a realistic enjoyment of good relationships. When I still need letters to convince me of my value, when I still need attention even after having told all my friends that I was going to "retreat" for half a year, then there is a good reason to question if I really want to be "alone with the Alone."

Still, I am deeply convinced that when I allow God to enter into my loneliness, when I allow him to let me know that I am loved far more deeply than I can imagine, only then can I give and receive real friendship and write letters free from seductive motivations. When I can say with Paul, "not I live, but Christ lives in me," then I no longer need to depend on the attention of others to have a sense of self. Because then I realize that my most important identity is the identity I have received as a grace of God and which has made me a participant in the divine life of God himself.

Meanwhile, it remains remarkable how little is said and written about letter writing as an important form of ministry. A good letter can change the day for someone in pain, can chase away feelings of resentment, can create a smile and bring joy to the heart. After all, a good part of the New Testament consists of letters, and some of the most profound insights are written down in letters between people who are attracted to each other by a deep personal affection. Letter writing is a very important art, especially for those who want to bring the good news.

Saturday, 27

A few days ago we finished *Or I'll Dress You in Mourning*, the book about the Spanish bullfighter. The last page describes the meeting between the thirty-two-year-old millionaire matador and Generalissimo Franco. In many ways it is a sad ending. A young man still hardly able to read or write has become just as distastefully wealthy as he was distastefully poor. He has not become a very

happy man. He reached a wealth and popularity far beyond his own wildest dreams, but somehow he has not
been able as yet to understand the real tragedy of his
country. With a naïve pride he let himself be photo-
graphed with Franco, the man who imprisoned his father
in his labor camps. Now we are reading *The Great Hunger*
by Cecil Woodham Smith. It is a detailed history of the
Irish potato famine of the 1840s which caused the death
of about a million peasants and was one of the major
stimuli of the great Irish emigration to the United States.
After hearing about poverty and hunger in Spain, now we
hear an even more detailed account of the suffering of the
Irish peasants during the last century.

Meanwhile, the papers keep us aware of the starvation
of the people in North Africa. I don't think that any monk
will have any illusions when he does a little bit of fasting.
The simple meals here start looking and even tasting like
luxurious banquets when you take in these hunger stories
together with your food.

One of the characteristics that the psycho-historian Bob
Lifton discerns in modern men and women is their historical dislocation. They miss that sense of continuity that is
so important for a creative life-style. They find themselves
part of a nonhistory in which only the sharp moment of
the here and now is valuable.

I was thinking about this when I read an article called,
"Quest for Identity: Americans go on a genealogy kick."
It says: "Many young people of the 'now generation' of
the 1960s who once voiced disinterest in a 'dead' past—are
joining the rush to find out: 'What is my past? Who are
my forbears? What were they like? What did they do?'
. . . Libraries and archives with genealogical holdings report that business is on the increase. At the National
Archives in Washington, D.C., written inquiries have
climbed from about 3,000 a month in 1954 to about 4,000
per week this year. In addition, nearly 1,000 people each
week come in person to search through a million cubic
feet of records."[18]

Something seems to be changing and changing fast. The mood at university campuses this year is strikingly different from three years ago. Less activistic, more reflective, less avant-garde, more traditional, less concerned with the "latest," more with the "earliest," less restless, more sedate. Some people speak about a return to the fifties. Maybe so, but it is more than that. For those who have lived through the sixties, the seventies will necessarily be different from the fifties. But we are certainly searching for our roots. I sense it in myself. Here I am first reading John of the Ladder, Evagrius, Dorotheus, Diadochus—men who wrote their works between 350 and 650—and now I am immersed in Bernard of Clairvaux, William of St. Thierry, and Aelred of Rievaulx, three great personalities of the twelfth century.

I feel very close to them. I feel that these "old men" help me immensely in my search for myself and my God. They do much more than remind me that my problems are not new and original. They give me a new sense of self, deeply embedded in the tumultuous history of God's people. I am not very interested in my genealogy, but maybe what I am doing and what many young people are doing in the Washington Archives is not so different after all: We are searching for our roots. For those who have heard little, if anything, about God's entry into history through his son, Jesus Christ, the Washington Archives are a quite understandable place to start looking for an answer to the question, "What is my past and what does that tell me about myself here and now?"

Sunday, 28

What do you do when you are always comparing yourself with other people? What do you do when you always feel that the people you talk to, hear of, or read about are more intelligent, more skillful, more attractive, more gentle, more generous, more practical, or more contemplative than you are? What do you do when you can't get away from measuring yourself against others, always feeling that they are the real people while you are a nobody or even less than that?

It is obvious that these feelings are distorted, out of proportion, the result of projections, and very damaging for a healthy spiritual life, but still they are no less real and can creep up on you before you are aware of it. Before you know it you are comparing other people's age and accomplishments with your own, and before you know it you have entered into a very harmful psychological competition and rivalry.

I talked about this with John Eudes today. He helped me analyze it a little more. We talked about the vicious circle one enters when one has a low self-esteem or self-doubt and then perceives other people in such a way as to strengthen and confirm these feelings. It is the famous self-fulfilling prophecy all over again. I enter into relationships with some apprehension and fear and behave in such a way that whatever the others say or do, I experience them as stronger, better, more valuable persons, and myself as weaker, worse, and not worth talking to. After a while the relationship becomes intolerable, and I find an excuse to walk away feeling worse than when I started it. My general abstract feeling of worthlessness becomes concrete in a specific encounter, and there my false fears increase rather than decrease. So real peer relationships become difficult, if not impossible, and many of my emotions in relation to others reveal themselves as the passive-dependent sort.

What do you do? Analyze more? It is not hard to see the neurotic dynamism. But it is not easy to break through it to a mature life. There is much to say about this and much has been said by psychologists and psychotherapists. But what to say about it from a spiritual perspective?

John Eudes talked about that moment, that point, that spot that lies before the comparison, before the beginning of the vicious circle or the self-fulfilling prophecy. That is the moment, point, or place where meditation can enter in. It is the moment to stop reading, speaking, socializing, and to "waste" your time in meditation. When you find your mind competing again, you might plan an "empty time" of meditation, in this way interrupting the vicious circle of your ruminations and entering into the depth of your own soul. There you can be with him who was before you came, who loved you before you could love, and who has given you your own self before any comparison was possible. In meditation we can come to the affirmation that we are not created by other people but by God, that we are not judged by how we compare with others but how we fulfill the will of God.

This is not as easy as it sounds because it is in meditation itself that we become painfully aware how much we have already been victimized by our own competitive strivings and how much we have already sold our soul to the opinions of others. By not avoiding this realization, however, but by confronting it and by unmasking its illusory quality, we might be able to experience our own basic dependency and so dispel the false dependencies of our daily life.

The more I think about this, the more I realize how central the words of St. John are, words so central also in St. Bernard's thought: "Let us love God because God has loved us first."

Monday, 29

Many contrasting emotions entered my heart today. Between the pages filled with news about the impeachment procedures in Washington, the New York *Times* "Week in Review" mentioned the happy news that the Greek military dictatorship had come to an end after its failure to bring Cyprus under its power, and that the new premier, Caramanlis, had released all political prisoners. I keep thinking about the joy of those men and women who suffered so dreadfully in the Greek prisons and who are now suddenly free. I keep seeing people embracing each other with tears of joy on the streets of Athens. Who could have dreamed a week ago that this was possible? How I hope that this will happen in Chile, Paraguay, and Brazil as well!

But also sad news. The news bulletin of the Fellowship of Reconciliation mentions that four Buddhist monks were shot to death and ten wounded in Kien Thanh in the South Vietnamese district of Kien Giang when police teargassed and fired upon two hundred demonstrating monks. This happened on June 6. No news from the many Buddhists in prison.

All the monks in the Abbey signed a petition to President Nixon asking for immediate and drastic measures to alleviate the hunger in North Africa and to prevent full-scale starvation. The petition, organized by "Bread for the World," asks the President to share our resources with hungry people everywhere, urges an immediate increase in food aid, and stresses the importance of building a world food security system. It also says, "We are willing to eat less to feed the hungry." I am happy that we can at least make our voices heard in this way. Maybe fasting can receive new meaning again, just in a period when Church laws on fasting have practically vanished outside the monastery.

Tuesday, 30

Whether it is good or bad I do not know, but there is no doubt that solitude leads me to think often about my past. The silent rhythm of the monastic life makes me explore my memory. I am amazed how little I remember. What did I do, think and feel between the ages of six and twelve? Little fragments come to mind. A friendly brother in the first grade who told a story about missionaries in Africa, a severe teacher in the sixth grade who one day invited all his students to his home, classmates laughing at me because I was cross-eyed, my first communion, the beginning of the war and my parents crying, the death of my grandmother and her funeral, Indian games and cowboy fights—but except for these flashes of memories, large empty periods. What happened during my teen-age years? How many names of classmates in high school do I remember? Where are they now? I am amazed by the big gaps and long stretches of time that seem void of memorable events. What in heaven's name did I do during those long six years in the seminary. I worked hard, but did I learn much?

Did I really live my life or was it lived for me? Did I really make the decisions that led me to this place at this time, or was I simply carried along by the stream, by sad as well as happy events? I do not want to live it all again, but I would like to remember more, so that my own little history could be a book to reflect on and learn from. I don't believe that my life is a long row of randomly chained incidents and accidents of which I am not much more than a passive victim. No, I think that nothing is accidental but that God molded me through the events of my life and that I am called to recognize his molding hand and praise him in gratitude for the great things he has done to me.

I wonder if I really have listened carefully enough to the God of history, the God of my history, and have recognized him when he called me by my name, broke the bread, or asked me to cast out my nets after a fruitless day? Maybe I have been living much too fast, too restlessly, too feverishly, forgetting to pay attention to what is happening here and now, right under my nose. Just as a whole world of beauty can be discovered in one flower, so the great grace of God can be tasted in one small moment. Just as no great travels are necessary to see the beauty of creation, so no great ecstasies are needed to discover the love of God. But you have to be still and wait so that you can realize that God is not in the earthquake, the storm, or the lightning, but in the gentle breeze with which he touches your back.

The weather today was splendid. Sunny, clear, cool, fresh, and joyful. I went bird watching for a while with John Eudes. We got caught in thorn apple bushes and our shoes got terribly muddy from walking through a freshly plowed field. We saw some nice killdeer in flight.

This afternoon I worked in the creek and found more granite rocks than usual. The purple loosestrife colored the edges of the creek. On our way back, Father Stephen pointed out to me the beautiful trees called sunburst locust. Within a few weeks they will "burst out" in yellow colors.

Wednesday, 31

Kevin's mother died. Kevin is a carpenter who lives with the Genesee Community. A few weeks ago he flew to Ireland to visit his mother who was fatally ill with diabetes. Last week he returned not knowing how long his mother could live.

The death of Kevin's mother brought back many memories of Donegal, the county where Kevin's family lives. I remember very vividly my hitchhike travels through the dark, melancholy hills of Northern Ireland. I wrote stories about the storytellers of Donegal in the Dutch newspapers and, while Kerry and Killarney left hardly any memories in my mind, Donegal I will never forget.

There was something somber but also profound and even holy about Donegal. The people were like the land. I still see vividly the simple funeral of a Donegal farmer. The priest and a few men carried the humble coffin to the cemetery. After the coffin was put in the grave, the men filled the grave with sand and covered it again with the patches of grass which had been laid aside. Two men stamped with their boots on the sod so that it was hardly possible to know that this was a grave. Then one of the men took two pieces of wood, bound them together in the form of a cross and stuck it in the ground. Everyone made a quick sign of the cross and left silently. No words, no solemnity, no decoration. Nothing of that. But it never has been made so clear to me that someone was dead, not asleep but dead, not passed away but dead, not laid to rest but dead, plain dead. When I saw those two men stamping on the ground in which they had buried their friend, I knew that for these farmers of Donegal there were no funeral-home games to play. But their realism became a transcendent realism by the simple unadorned wooden cross saying that where death is affirmed, hope finds its roots. "Unless a wheat grain falls on the ground and dies, it remains only a single grain; but if it dies, it yields a rich harvest" (Jn. 12:24).

The Mass we celebrated for Kevin's mother was simple and beautiful. Kevin came afterward to shake hands with the celebrant and concelebrants. All the way through the ceremony I saw the simple men of Donegal digging their grave and sticking their cross in the ground. "Margaret, may she dwell in the house of the Lord . . ."

CHAPTER THREE

AUGUST

Nixon and St. Bernard

AUGUST

Friday, 2

The evening prayers called Compline (meaning: to make
the day complete) form one of the most intimate moments
of the monastic day. It is the moment during which all the
monks are present, even those who sometimes have to be
absent during other prayers, and during which you sense
a real togetherness. The prayers are always the same.
Therefore, nobody needs a book. Everyone can stand
wherever he wants, and therefore no lights are necessary.
All is quiet in the house. It is the beginning of what the
monks call the great silence which lasts from 6:30 P.M.
until 5:30 A.M.

Compline is such an intimate and prayerful moment
that some people in the neighborhood come daily to the
Abbey to join in this most quiet prayer of the day.

I start realizing that the psalms of Compline slowly become flesh in me; they become part of my night and lead
me to a peaceful sleep.

Ponder on your bed and be still:
Make justice your sacrifice and trust in the Lord.

I will lie down in peace and sleep comes at once
for You alone, Lord, make me dwell in safety (Ps. 4).

Trust is written all through the evening prayer:

He who dwells in the shelter of the Most High
and abides in the shade of the Almighty
says to the Lord: "My refuge,
my stronghold, my God in whom I trust!"

It is he who will free you from the snare
of the fowler who seeks to destroy you;
he will conceal you with his pinions
and under his wings you will find refuge (Ps. 90).

Slowly these words enter into the center of my heart. They are more than ideas, images, comparisons: They become a real presence. After a day with much work or with many tensions, you feel that you can let go in safety and realize how good it is to dwell in the shelter of the Most High.

Many times I have thought: If I am ever sent to prison, if I am ever subjected to hunger, pain, torture, or humiliation, I hope and pray that they let me keep the psalms. The psalms will keep my spirit alive, the psalms will allow me to comfort others, the psalms will prove the most powerful, yes, the most revolutionary weapon against the oppressor and torturer. How happy are those who no longer need books but carry the psalms in their heart wherever they are and wherever they go. Maybe I should start learning the psalms by heart so that nobody can take them away from me. Just to be able to say over and over again:

O men, how long will your hearts be closed, will you love what is futile and seek what is false?

It is the Lord who grants favors to those whom he loves; the Lord hears me whenever I call him (Ps. 4).

That is a prayer that really can heal many wounds.

Yesterday they started to lay the foundations for the new church. Amazing how fast it all goes. What was a piece of flat ground is now opened up by deep trenches, and already concrete has been poured into the wooden forms. Monks were watching silently as the large machines did their work and young men shouted orders to each other. Building a shelter for the Most High.

This morning I kicked over a big pile of boxes with freshly washed raisins. It was a real mess. But nobody seemed upset. "That has happened before," Brother Theodore said. Then he turned on the machine and washed them again.

Monday, 5

Today I read *Living and Dying* by Robert Jay Lifton and Eric Olson. One theme hit me with new force. Speaking about the survivors of the Hiroshima atomic explosion, they write: "Among the survivors there quickly developed a profound kind of guilt. This guilt was related both to having remained alive while others (including loved ones and neighbors) died and to the inability to offer help to those who needed it. All of this became focused in a question that remained at the center of a life struggle for the survivors: 'Why did I remain alive when he, she, they died?' And this question itself sometimes became transformed into the haunting suspicion that one's own life had been purchased at the cost of the others who died: 'Some had to die; because they died I could live.' This suspicion led to a feeling among survivors that they did not deserve to be alive and that one could justly remain alive only by coming in some way to resemble the dead."[1] The great all-pervasive idea of the book is formulated in the state-

ment: ". . . we are all survivors of this century's holo-
causts."

Although I had read this before, it struck me with new
force because I started to wonder how far my preoccupation with those who suffer and die in prisons all over
the world and my growing concern about the millions who
starve in North Africa are tainted by this survivors' guilt?
"Why them, why not me?" "Why the poor and not the
prosperous?" Behind all of that lurks the question: "Is
there a way to become part of their pain to justify my
own being alive?"

. I oiled a few thousand bread pans this morning. Noisy
work but not too bad.

Tuesday, 6

Today: the great feast of the Transfiguration. A silent
hermit day. After the simple liturgy in the chapter room
everyone went his own way into the silence.

I read Merton's article on the Pasternak affair[2] and
parts from Pasternak's *I Remember* and *Doctor Zhivago.* I
am surprised to find a beautiful story about Psalm 90. It
tells how Dr. Zhivago found the text of this psalm on the
bodies of two soldiers, one a Red partisan, the other a
White Russian volunteer: the first dead, the second
wounded. Pasternak writes: "The text was believed to be
miraculous and a protection against bullets. It has been
worn as a talisman by soldiers in the latest imperialist
war. Decades later prisoners were to sew it into their
clothes and mutter its words in jail when they were sum-
moned at night for interrogation."[3]

> You will not fear the terror of night
> nor the arrow that flies by day,
> nor the plague that prowls in the darkness
> nor the scourge that lays waste at noon (Ps. 90:5–6).

Russian soldiers prayed it, Red and White, monks pray it, black and white, I pray it—I'd better learn it by heart so that I don't need to sew it in my clothes and so that it can become ingrained in my innermost being.

The House Judiciary Committee voted (all Democrats [twenty-one] and seven Republicans) to recommend to the House of Representatives that President Nixon be impeached. It is the event that will dominate the news during the summer.

Wednesday, 7

During Sext, the short communal prayer before dinner, Brother Alberic came into the church making a gesture that caused about half of the monks to walk out of church as fast as they could. The others, myself included, stayed, not knowing what was going on. We finished our prayers and went to the dining hall to eat. During dinner the others returned and it became clear that the straw in the field had caught fire and that a few men were needed to extinguish it.

I spent the afternoon with Brother Henry at his beehives. This was my first encounter with the bees. Although I was well protected, one bee found its way into one of the legs of my pants. Well, he stung and died as a hero. A remarkable world. Now I am reading up on bees: Murray Hoyt's book, *The World of Bees*. There I found an example of American pragmatism that makes you cry. Based on the biblical expression of Israel as the "land flowing with milk and honey," Professor Mykola H. Haydak wanted to test whether this were the perfect diet combination. After two months on a diet of milk and honey, "his skin became dry, pimples marred his face and whitish round spots appeared on his tongue"—the obvious result of lack of vitamin C. "He added ten ounces of or-

ange juice a day and all these symptoms disappeared."
Hoyt remarks after describing the experiment: "So perhaps the 'land flowing with milk and honey' should be
changed to 'a land flowing with milk and honey and ten
ounces of orange juice.'"[4]

Friday, 9

When Christian writes a note to me or to anyone, he always marks a little cross on top of the page. This morning
while I had my head deep in the tub of raisins, he came
over to the bakery and handed me one of his notes. There
was the little cross and under it: "Nixon resigned."

In the afternoon I drove to Rochester to see the dentist.
The doctor had a T.V. set placed high up in a corner of
his office so that his patients could watch it while he was
watching their bad teeth. At noon they had seen the
inauguration of the new President, Gerald Ford, half an
hour after the Nixon family had left the White House.
The picture of a patient watching the inauguration of the
new President of the U.S.A. with open mouth in a dentist's chair stuck in my mind as quite appropriate for the
occasion.

Saturday, 10

Worked with John Eudes and Brian in Salt Creek collecting stones. Brian drove the pickup truck right into the
creek to load it up with stones. While he was driving the
loaded truck out of the water with all four wheels en-
gaged, the truck jumped so badly that half the load rolled
out again and the old rusted fender nearly broke off. We
reloaded the truck, pulled the thing out of the water, and
came safely home in time for a shower before Vespers.

Sunday, 11

After my visit to Rochester, a passage from Merton's *Conjectures of a Guilty Bystander*, which John Eudes quoted in Chapter had a special meaning to me. It speaks about one of Merton's trips to Louisville: "In Louisville, at the corner of Fourth and Walnut, in the center of the shopping district, I was suddenly overwhelmed with the realization that I loved all those people, that they were mine and I theirs, that we could not be alien to one another even though we were total strangers . . . though 'out of the world' [monks] are in the same world as everybody else, the world of the bomb, the world of race hatred, the world of technology, the world of mass media, big business, revolution and all the rest. We take a different attitude to all these things, for we belong to God. Yet so does everybody else belong to God. We just happen to be conscious of it and make a profession out of this consciousness. But does that entitle us to consider ourselves different, or even *better*, than others? The whole idea is preposterous . . .

"I have the immense joy of being *man*, a member of a race in which God himself became incarnate. As if the sorrows and stupidities of the human condition could overwhelm me, now I realize what we all are. And if only everybody could realize this! But it cannot be explained. There is no way of telling people that they are all walking around shining like the sun.

"This changes nothing in the sense and value of my solitude, for it is in fact the function of solitude to make one realize such things with a clarity that would be impossible to anyone completely immersed in the other cares, the other illusions, and all the automatisms of a tightly collective existence. My solitude, however, is not my own, for I see how much it belongs to them—and that I have a responsibility for it in their regard, not just in my own. It is because I am one with them that I owe it to them to be alone, and when I am alone, they are not 'they' but my own self. There are no strangers!"[5]

Rochester is to Genesee what Louisville is to Gethsemani. Merton wrote this after more than fifteen years in the monastery. Still—after only nine weeks in the monastery—I had similar feelings when I was in Rochester. When I walked into a flower shop to buy some white and yellow chrysanthemums for friends in town I felt a deep love for the florist who, with a twinkle in his eye, told me that chrysanthemums were "year-round flowers," not bound to the seasons. I felt open, free, and relaxed and really enjoyed the little conversation we had on flowers, presidents, and honesty in politics.

I am becoming more and more aware that solitude indeed makes you more sensitive to the good in people and even enables you to bring it to the foreground. No, "there is no way of telling people that they are all walking around shining like the sun" but God's glory in you can bring out God's glory in the other when you have become more conscious of this shared gift. God speaks to God, Spirit to Spirit, Love to Love. It is all a gift, it is all grace.

Monday, 12

I told John Eudes today that I felt that the past week had been somewhat "bourgeois." My mind had been focused more on the news than on other things, and I had settled in a somewhat comfortable pattern of living which, as far as its spiritual content is concerned, is not so different from my previous life. I said that I felt the temptation to make the monastic life a comfortable, settled existence without much challenge and that I realized that this, in fact, meant that religion then is just a commodity and no longer a spiritual adventure.

John Eudes laughed a little and said that it showed on the one hand that I had started to feel at home and that is a good thing, but on the other hand that indeed there was "work" to be done. Then he said, "But don't worry. It won't last long this way. This is the time in which meditation becomes very important; this is an invitation to enter deeper into prayer. Otherwise, you will start complaining within a few weeks that the monastery is not severe enough, not poor enough, not strict enough, and you, as many others before, will leave and start a life which, in fact, is much less poor and less severe."

Speaking about prayer, I asked John Eudes a question that seemed very basic and a little naïve: "When I pray, to whom do I pray?" "When I say 'Lord,' what do I mean?"

John Eudes responded very differently than I expected. He said, "This is the real question, this is the most important question you can raise; at least this is the question that you can make your most important question." He stressed with great and convincing emphasis that if I really wanted to take that question seriously, I should realize that there would be little room left for other things. "Except," he said smiling, "when the question exhausts you so much that you need to read *Newsweek* for a little relaxation!" "It is far from easy," John Eudes said, "to make that question the center of your meditation. You will discover that it involves every part of yourself because the question, Who is the Lord to whom I pray? leads directly to the question, Who am I who wants to pray to the Lord? And then you will soon wonder, Why is the Lord of justice also the Lord of love; the God of fear also the God of gentle compassion? This leads you to the center of meditation. Is there an answer? Yes and no. You will find out in your meditation. You might some day have a flash of understanding even while the question still remains and pulls you closer to God. But it is not a question that can be simply one of your questions. In a way, it needs to be your only question around which all that you do finds its place. It requires a certain decision to make that question the center of your meditation. If you do so, you will real-

ize that you are embarking on a long road, a very long
road."

Tuesday, 13

This morning Father John explained to me that the killdeer is a bird that fools you by simulating injury to pull
your attention away from her eggs which she lays openly
on a sandy place. Beautiful! Neurosis as weapon! How
often I have asked pity for a very unreal problem in order
to pull people's attention away from what I didn't want
them to see.

Sometimes it seems that every bird has institutionalized
one of my defense mechanisms. The cowbird lays her eggs
in some other bird's nest to let them do the brooding job;
the Baltimore oriole imitates the sounds of more dangerous birds to keep the enemies away, and the red-wing
blackbird keeps screaming so loudly overhead that you
get tired of her noise and soon leave the area that she con-
siders hers. It does not take long to realize that I do all of
that and a lot more to protect myself or to get my own
will done.

Thursday, 15

The feast of Our Lady's Assumption is an important
feast for monks because under this title Mary is the pa-
troness of all the monks. I didn't understand this well
enough when I came here, but the longer I am here, the
more I realize that Mary is for the monks the most pure
contemplative. Luke describes her as contemplating the
mysteries of the redemption. After telling about the visit
of the shepherds to the Child, he writes: "As for Mary,
she treasured all these things and pondered them in her
heart" (Lk. 2:19), and after describing how she found

Jesus in the temple among the doctors of law, he adds:
"His mother stored up all these things in her heart." She
is the contemplative of whom the aged Simeon says that a
sword will pierce her soul (Lk. 2:35).

The doctrine of her Assumption affirms the fulfillment
of this contemplative life in heaven. There the most redeemed human being, the woman in whom God touched
us in the most intimate way, the mother of Jesus and all
who believe in him—there she stands in the presence of
God, enjoying forever the beatific vision that is the hope
of all monks and all Christians.

Brother James entered the novitiate today, after six
months of postulancy. He is one of those exceptional people who seem transparent in their openness, simplicity,
and prayerfulness. A hard-working, honest, straightforward farmer "incapable of deceit" (Jn. 1:47). When the
ceremony was supposed to start, he was the only one
who had not arrived yet. The novice master went out
looking for him and when he was found and in his
seat, the abbot said dryly, "Since we are all here, I guess
we can start."

It is an honor to be around a man like James. He
teaches me more about single-minded commitment than
many books. He read the Magnificat and other texts relating to Mary as "his texts" and when he came to the
words: "the Almighty has done great things to me," he
looked up from his little piece of paper and straight in his
brothers' faces. It was a moving moment. Now he is all
white. He walks in his new habit with the same somewhat
dragging gait as he did in his old one, but something new
has happened to him, and he knows it.

Friday, 16

"If I see three oranges, I have to juggle. And if I see
two towers, I have to walk." These remarkable words

were spoken by the tightrope-walker, Philippe Petit, in answer to the question of the police as to why he had walked (at 7:50 A.M.) on a rope shot with a crossbow from one tower of the New York World Trade Center to the other. When Philippe had seen the two spires of the Notre Dame in Paris, he had done the same. *"L'Art pour l'Art"* is this highwire artist's philosophy.

I have been thinking today, off and on, about this beautiful man Philippe Petit. His answer to the police is priceless and deserves long meditation. We always want answers to impossible questions. Why do you love her? Any answer to such a question is usually ridiculous. Because she is beautiful? Because she is intelligent? Because she has a funny pimple on her nose? Nothing makes much sense. Why did you become a priest? Because you love God? Because you like to preach? Because you don't like women? Why did you become a monk? Because you like to pray? Because you like silence? Because you like to bake bread without being bothered? There are no answers to those questions.

When they asked Philippe Petit why he wanted to walk on a slender wire strung between the two tallest towers of New York City, everyone thought he did it for money, for publicity, for fame. But he said, "If I see three oranges, I have to juggle. And if I see two towers, I have to walk."

We don't believe the most meaningful answer. We think that this man must be insane. In fact, they took Philippe to a city hospital for psychiatric examination but soon found out that Philippe was as healthy as could be. "Sane and ebullient," says the newspaper.

His is the true answer. Why do you love her? When I saw her, I loved her. Why are you a priest? Because I must be a priest. Why do you pray? Because when I see God, I must pray. There is an inner must, an inner urge, or inner call that answers all those questions which are beyond explanation. Never does anyone who asks a monk why he became a monk receive a satisfying answer. Nor do children give us an explanation when we ask them, "Why do you play ball?" They know that there is no answer except, "When I see a ball, I have to play with it."

The police who arrested Philippe Petit seemed to understand this because they dropped the original charge of trespassing and disorderly conduct in exchange for Philippe's promise to perform his aerial feats for the children in Central Park. That at least brought some real humanity back into the picture. Meanwhile, I keep saying to myself, "If I see three oranges, I have to juggle. And if I see two towers, I have to walk."

Saturday, 17

After a series of dry, sunny days, the rain poured down this morning with much vehemence and noise. It was a special sensation to walk through this low-built, barracklike monastery and see and hear the water on all sides while remaining dry and comfortable. Many people in this country and elsewhere in this world are waiting for it. Here it has been coming at regular intervals and has brought about a very good wheat harvest.

In the afternoon John Eudes, Brian, Robert—a new observer—and I went to the creek to collect more stones. From the flat wagon drawn by the tractor, the land looked very beautiful. A mysterious veil covered the fields just harvested, and the gentle hills of New York State seemed grateful for the moist air and showed themselves in a new beauty. I felt happy and grateful and kept thinking an old thought: I wished that all my friends whom I love so much could see and feel what I can see and feel today. But I know they never will. On this earth the experience of great beauty always remains mysteriously linked with the experience of great loneliness. This reminds me again that there still is a beauty I have not seen yet: the beauty that does not create loneliness but unity.

Theodore found a little piece of metal between the

thousands of raisins he pushed through the raisin washing machine. He showed it to me. It looked as sharp as a razor blade. Well, someone eating his raisin bread is saved from a bleeding stomach, thanks to Theodore, who will never hear a grateful word for it. That is the drawback of preventive medicine.

Sunday, 18

Liturgically this was quite a violent Sunday. During Vigils, the communal night prayer at 2:30 A.M., we heard the word of Yahweh through his prophet Joel:

> Proclaim this among the nations,
> "Prepare for war!
> Muster the champions!
> Warriors, advance,
> quick march!
> Hammer your plowshares into swords,
> your sickles into spears,
> let the weakling say, 'I am a fighting man!'"
> (Jl. 4:9–10)

During Mass we first heard how Jeremiah was thrown by his enemies into a cistern. "There was no water in the well, only mud, and into the mud Jeremiah sank" (Jer. 38:6). Then the writer of the letter to the Hebrews says: "Think of the way he [Christ] stood such opposition from sinners and then you will not give up for want of courage" (Heb. 12:4). Finally, we heard the words of Jesus: "Do you suppose that I am here to bring peace on earth? No, I tell you, but rather division" (Lk. 12:51).

This is a side of the Bible I tend to forget. But the Bible is a realistic book and does not avoid any part of human reality. It speaks about the life, thoughts, and history of men and women from the perspective of the God of history. It is good to be reminded of this realism. God is not only where it is peaceful and quiet but also where there is persecution, struggle, division, and conflict. God, indeed, did not promise us a rose garden.

Monday, 19

The news in the New York *Times*, the letters from India posted on the bulletin board and the increasing requests for money, food, and clothes give me more and more the feeling that I belong to the happy few allowed into the Ark of Noah. The comparison does not work too well with all these celibates, but I keep thinking about sitting on the top of a mountain while the world around me is washed away. While we have a very abundant wheat crop, the papers speak about floods in India washing away whole crops and about droughts in North Africa and parts of the U.S.A. creating endless misery there and inflation here. While we have healthy, strong-looking men here, the pictures show emaciated people floating nowhere on self-made rafts. While we have peace and an atmosphere of trust here, in Cyprus, Greece, Chile, Brazil, the Middle East, South Korea, etc. hostilities break out everyday. Still I often feel homesick for the world with its pains and problems.

Sometimes the mentioning of a prayer intention becomes like a news service. Father Marcellus said during Vespers, "Let us pray for the wife of the President of South Korea"—then he realized that nobody except he had read the latest newspaper, and quickly added—"who was assassinated"—then it probably flashed through his mind that nobody could understand why anyone would want to assassinate the wife of the President of South Korea, so he added—"while someone was trying to assassinate the President himself"—then he realized that by now the monks wanted to know the end of the story, so he concluded his intention with the words—"who safely escaped."

That is what happens when you are librarian and read the paper first!

Tuesday, 20

Feast of St. Bernard. The liturgy was filled with gentle, sometimes sweet, compliments to this great saint of the twelfth century. During the night Office, one of his sermons was read. Simplicity, soberness, and austerity were Bernard's ideals. He practiced them too, but his language is wealthy, decorative, ornate, playful, and nearly baroque. His sermons on the Song of Songs belong to the classics of world literature but certainly not because of their sobriety!

Brian celebrated his feast day. I didn't understand. First, I thought that Brian was the name of an Irish Saint. Wrong. There simply is no Saint Brian. Only a famous King Brian. Dom James Fox, who was abbot of Gethsemani when Brian entered there, told him that "Brian" was Gaelic for "Bernard," that he was to be called "Brian," and that his feast day would be that of St. Bernard, August 20. Well, Brian obeyed and that was that. Today the monks prayed especially for their brother Brian.

Wednesday, 21

Yesterday I stumbled over a book, which made me feel that God had put it in my way so that I would pick it up and read it. The book is called *A Passion for Truth*. It is the last book by Abraham Joshua Heschel, which he delivered to his publisher a few weeks before his death.

When I read Heschel, I often have the same feeling of being "at home" as when I read Thomas Merton. Both seem to speak a language that has an easiness and obviousness which I miss with other spiritual writers. They both seem to speak directly to me and very little, if any, "translation" seems necessary.

During the last weeks I have become increasingly aware that my diary shows a strong contrast between notes on the joy of God's presence, the silence and quietude of the monastery, the love of the monks, the beauty of nature, and notes on hunger in Africa and India, torture in Chile, Brazil, Vietnam, wars everywhere, and the general state of misery of the world. It almost seems as if there were two persons in me experiencing life quite differently, praying differently, and listening differently. I started to wonder how they both could live together in peace.

In the introduction to his book *A Passion for Truth*, Heschel explains why he had to write this book. He tells how two figures played a great role in his youth and continuing spiritual life: The Baal Shem Tov and Reb Menahem Mendl of Kotzk, both representing a real part of himself. The Baal Shem Tov, the father of Hassidism, represented his experience of peace, joy, beauty, while Menahem Mendl represented anxiety, restless search, austere denial of self. Heschel writes: ". . . I realized that in being guided by both the Baal Shem Tov and the Kotzker [Menahem Mendl], I had allowed two forces to carry on a struggle within me. . . . In a very strange way, I found my soul at home with the Baal Shem but driven by the Kotzker. Was it good to live with one's heart torn between the joy of Mezbizh [the Baal Shem Tov] and the anxiety of Kotzk? . . . I had no choice; my heart was in Mezbizh, my mind in Kotzk. I was taught about the inexhaustible mines of meaning by the Baal Shem; from the Kotzker I learned to detect immense mountains of absurdity standing in the way. . . . The one reminded me that there could be a Heaven on earth, the other shocked me into discovering Hell in the alleged Heavenly places in our world. . . . The Baal Shem dwelled in my life like a lamp, while the Kotzker struck like lightning. To be sure, lightning is more authentic. Yet one can trust a lamp, put confidence in it; one can live in peace with a lamp. The Baal Shem gave me wings; the Kotzker encircled me with chains. I never had the courage to break the chains and entered into joys with my shortcomings in mind. I owe intoxication to the Baal Shem, to the Kotzker the blessings of humiliation."[6]

It says it all. So powerful and clear. Just to see these tensions expressed by Heschel gives me a great sense of being accepted.

I saw two monks having a lively discussion in sign language. Their rapid hand and arm movements made it quite a scene to see. Just when I was wondering what they were talking about, I recognized the signs saying, "Let's go into that room there so we can talk about it." Sign language obviously has its limits.

Thursday, 22

Brother Alexis, the bookkeeper, induced me to buy a stapler with ball-point pen and ruler under one plastic cover, all for $.96! I didn't really need any of it, but he made me feel that without it something would go wrong in my life. Brother Alexis is a great salesman, and since I am the only real buyer in this place, he practices his skills on me.

He has a sharp eye for "good buys" and saves all the ads announcing special sales with reduced prices. Then when the time is ripe, he has someone run to the stores to buy enormous quantities of it, probably leaving the store owner under the impression that his article is very popular and that he made a mistake by reducing the price. But in a place like this anything gets used some day, some week, some year, by someone. The Trappist order certainly won't collapse from a lack of Scotch tape and ball-point

pens. Brother Alexis has hundreds of feet of the one and
an endless amount of the other.

I have a stapler now and it works as long as you don't
expect miracles of it. When you want to staple more than
five pages together at once, it will probably develop a
fatal illness and collapse with a squeak. But what greedy
man wants to staple more than five pages together?

Friday, 23

I got trapped today by the new Encyclopaedia Britan-
nica. This is the fifteenth edition of the E.B.—the 1974 edition. It had just arrived in the library and a note on the
bulletin board had invited us to take a look at this new-
comer. I just wanted to have a quick look and ended up
staying two hours playing with the thirty volumes. It is indeed a sort of game.

I looked up "Christ" in the Micropaedia. It said: "See
Jesus of Nazareth." God became a name among other
names. In this context, Jesuits come earlier than Jesus of
Nazareth!

Saturday, 24

While pressing what seemed to me about two hundred
bed sheets, my fellow worker told me about his decision
to enter the monastery.

Coming from an Oriental family with very close family
ties, his desire to go to a Christian monastery not only was
not supported but was criticized and never understood. "I
never could explain it to them," he said with a certain
sadness. "When I told them that I would never come
home again, not even on the day of my parents' funeral,
they just couldn't accept it." It must have been a great
struggle. His deep family loyalty made him feel like his

parents and brothers, but at the same time, the monastery kept calling him, nearly against his own desire. "I delayed for five years," he said. "When I prayed, I said, 'Tomorrow, Lord, tomorrow, not today, not yet.'" Finally he went.

When his father died, he did not go home and every year when his mother came to the monastery, she came to take him with her. Now seventy-five years old, she has accepted the fact that her son will not return to the family. She accepts it but still doesn't understand. There is only one consolation for her. When she dies, her son will come to the funeral. A change in rules has made this possible. The Orientals feel that whoever the Christian God is, he cannot be a good God if he does not want children to bury their parents. Today it seems that the Trappists feel the same.

Sunday, 25

If there is any good way to get rid of the desire to become famous, it is by reading the book *Return to Earth* by the astronaut Buzz Aldrin. The book arrived two days ago and I find it very telling. The book doesn't speak much about the moon trip, but talks mostly about the life of the Aldrin family after the trip was over. I remember watching Aldrin on T.V. in Chile as he set foot on the moon. Some Chileans in the poor section of town were afraid that something terrible would happen when the astronauts stepped on the moon. They considered it a sacrilegious act. Well, something terrible happened—not what some Chileans expected, but the growing unhappiness of the man who touched the moon. I have to read more.

Monday, 26

Talked with John Eudes about obedience. I said, "I don't think I ever could become a monk because of my problem with obedience. If you or anyone else told me to go collect stones every day while I was deeply convinced that I should write, read, study, or whatever, I would not be able to take it and would become so restless and hostile that I would leave sooner or later."

He said, "The reasons you give not only would make you a poor monk but also a poor diocesan priest. Your problem is not that specific for monks. If you cannot be detached from all you do and like to do, you cannot live a full spiritual life."

So we talked about obedience. It was helpful because John Eudes made me see that the problem of obedience is a problem of intimacy. "Obedience becomes hard when you have to be vulnerable to the other who has authority. You can play the obedience game in such a way that you never disobey any rule while keeping from your guide and director, your abbot or superior those things about which you do not want to hear a "no." You need a lot of trust to give yourself fully to someone else, certainly to someone to whom you owe obedience. Many people adapt very quickly but are not really obedient. They simply don't want to make waves and instead go along with the trend. That is not obedience. That is just adaptation."

If I were able to trust more, to open myself more easily, to be more vulnerable, then obedience would not be so hard. I would be able to disagree without fear of rejection, to protest without resentment, to express different viewpoints without self-righteousness, and to say after all arguments: "If I am still asked to do something I do not like to do, perhaps I must be open to the idea of God's preparing me for something greater and more important than I can imagine."

With that attitude, life in obedience indeed can be quite exciting since you never really know what is next. But I have a long way to go to develop that attitude in my innermost self.

Wednesday, 28

My dreams are getting wilder and wilder. Last night I dreamed that I was sitting on a bench covered by a soft mattress that was attached to the outside railing of the Golden Gate Bridge in San Francisco. The bench moved gently from one side of the bay to the other, giving me a fantastic view of the water underneath with ocean liners and sailboats and of the clear sky above me with little sheeplike clouds. Slowly I moved toward the city which was beautifully white with impressive clean buildings and high skyscrapers.

My friends, Don and Claude, welcomed me when I arrived at the city and took me to a big hotel where we went to the bar and had a most pleasant conversation with the bartender. In fact, he liked us so much that he showed us the parts of the hotel reserved for those with special club membership. He had the keys of all the doors and showed us the different luxurious meeting rooms. As we walked around, I saw a group of well-dressed men leaving for another location with wall-to-wall carpeting and lounge chairs.

When the bartender led us back to the lounge of the hotel, I noticed a group of Trappist priests in their white habits and black scapulars. They told me that they were going to say mass for the different key clubs. I was very angry with this religious support of elitist segregation and discrimination but did not protest and just left with Don and Claude.

Quite a revealing dream, I thought. While during the day I try to be in the world without being of it, during the night I am fully of it without really being in it.

Thursday, 29

At times, writing becomes a real event. During the last few days I have been worrying about how to write on the prayer of the heart. I reread different books on the prayer tradition of the desert fathers and went over the excerpts I had made earlier, but I still felt uneasy, not really ready to write. Today I simply decided to start and see what would happen. After the second sentence, it seemed as if my pen pulled me into a totally different direction than I had expected, and while I wrote one page after another, I realized that my concentration on the desert fathers had kept me from thinking and writing about more important things which fit much better into the totality of the book I am trying to write.

It was a remarkable sensation to see ideas and words flowing so easily, as if they had always been there but had not been allowed expression.

Meanwhile, I become more and more aware that for me writing is a very powerful way of concentrating and of clarifying for myself many thoughts and feelings. Once I put my pen on paper and write for an hour or two, a real sense of peace and harmony comes to me. Consequently, I feel much more willing and able to do little routine jobs. After a day without any writing and filled with only reading and manual work, I often have a general feeling of mental constipation and go to bed with the sense that I did not do what I should have done that day.

It is good to become aware of all this. This seems to help me to understand quite a few of my bad moods in New Haven during the past few years.

Friday, 30

This was one of those days that pass with many distractions and few real events. I washed raisins for more than four hours without even finishing the whole job, received a lot of mail that needed immediate attention, talked for a few hours with one of the guests who asked for some help in his life. Finally, I read that depressing weekly, *U. S. News and World Report,* which is obviously written for businessmen and not for monks.

In fact, this was a "typical" day when I think about my life before I came here. Busy, active, talkative, but very superficial and without much concentration on anything. It seems good to avoid more of such "typical days."

Saturday, 31

Writing about prayer is often very painful since it makes you so aware of how far away you are from the ideal you write about. People who read your ideas tend to think that your writings reflect your life. The only advantage of that is that your readers become your counselors and guides. They invite you and challenge you to live up to your own thoughts and insights.

This week all I am reading and writing about is prayer. I am so busy with it and often so excited about it that I have no time left to pray, and when I pray, I feel more drawn to my ideas on prayer than to praying.

While it is true that in order to pray you have to empty your heart and mind for God, you also have to empty your heart and mind of your feelings and ideas on prayer. Otherwise, prayer gets in the way of praying.

I have a strong feeling that my intellectual formation is just as much a hindrance as a help to prayer. It is hard

not to desire good insights during prayer and not to fall
into a long inner discussion with myself. Every time some
kind of insight comes to me, I find myself wondering how
I can use it in a lecture, a sermon, or an article, and very
soon I am far away from God and all wrapped up in my
own preoccupations. Maybe this is what makes the Jesus
Prayer so good for me. Simply saying, "Lord Jesus Christ,
have mercy on me" a hundred times, a thousand times,
ten thousand times, as the Russian peasant did, might
slowly clean my mind and give God a little chance.

CHAPTER FOUR

SEPTEMBER

Pray for the World

SEPTEMBER

Sunday, 1

Today starts my fourth month here. The idea that there are only four months left makes me apprehensive. Where will I be when Christmas comes around? But why ask such questions? "There is no need to worry," says St. Paul, "but if there is anything you need, pray for it, asking God for it with prayer and thanksgiving, and that peace of God, which is so much greater than we can understand, will guard your hearts and your thoughts in Christ Jesus" (Ph. 4:6–7). That must be enough for me.

Yesterday I received a letter asking for an article on the Holy Spirit. I answered that it seems better not to accept the invitation so that I might keep as faithful as possible to my retreat plans. But this morning, during my meditation, I found myself wondering what I could have written, and I got very involved in all kinds of "exciting" ideas on the Holy Spirit. When I woke up from my mental wandering, I said to myself, "Don't let yourself get distracted by thoughts about the Holy Spirit, but pray!" Then I had to laugh at the realization that the Holy Spirit got in his own

way. How complicated can you get! But filling your mind
with ideas about an article on the Holy Spirit is quite
different from emptying your mind so that the Holy Spirit
can pray in you. It is a difference as great as that between
speaking about God and speaking with him. It seems to
me that all asceticism starts with the recognition of this
difference and becomes a real task when you want to *live*
its implications. It is hard but not depressing, difficult but
challenging as well.

Father Stephen celebrated his fiftieth birthday today.
An intention during Vespers offered the information. I had
never realized that he was older than I. Monks look young
and Father Stephen even youthful. But like all of us, he
too is aging. His great zeal in collecting stones fills me
with a growing admiration for him. He really makes a vocation out of that job. When he goes out with his men to
collect stones he means business. To be "a rolling stone"
at this age is quite an accomplishment!

Monday, 2

In meditation today I read: ". . . prayer must be
sought with no scant effort: then God, seeing our travail,
will give us what we seek. True prayer will not be
achieved by human efforts: it is a gift of God. Seek and
you will find."[1] ". . . one must remember that success in
any aspect of the spiritual life is the fruit of the grace of
God. Spiritual life comes entirely from his most holy
Spirit. We have our own spirit but it is void of power. It
begins to gain strength only when the grace of God flows
into it."[2]
I wonder if depression in the spiritual life does not
mean that we have forgotten that prayer is grace. The
deep realization that all the fruits of the spiritual life are
gifts of God should make us smile, and liberate us from
any deadly seriousness. We can close our eyes as tightly

as we can and clasp our hands as firmly as possible, but God speaks only when he wants to speak. When we realize this our pressing, pushing, and pulling become quite amusing. Sometimes we act like a child that closes his eyes and thinks that he can make the world go away.

After having done everything to make some space for God, it is still God who comes on his own initiative. But we have a promise upon which to base our hope: The promise of his love. So our life can rightly be a waiting in expectation, but waiting patiently and with a smile. Then, indeed, we shall be really surprised and full of joy and gratitude when he comes.

Today I received a message saying that next Monday morning I have to appear at the Immigration and Naturalization office in Connecticut to obtain permanent residence in the U.S.A. That will take me away from here for a day and home for a night.

Wednesday, 4

After three months of manual work, I am realizing that I do not really enjoy it. When the novelty of it is gone, it becomes very boring. Packing bread, taking hot bread from the conveyor belt, washing raisins, pressing sheets, or collecting stones are all good jobs for one or two afternoons, but after three months my main question during work becomes: "When is this over?" The only thing that can take some of the dullness away is a good-natured co-worker.

I told all this to John Eudes because I felt it was important to wonder how I could make my work more a part of my prayer and not just an occasion to fret. John Eudes could well understand my feelings. To my amazement he said that many, in fact most, monks, especially the older ones, really enjoyed their work and did not feel as I do. I had been wondering about that. John Eudes showed me that this type of work gives me a good occasion to feel deeply my unrelatedness. In other situations I have intellectual defenses and strong repressions which prevent me from really feeling fully my unrelatedness. When I study, write, or lecture, I can make things interesting by manipulating them in certain ways. But in the bakery or in the creek, it is practically impossible to make things interesting. Then I am faced with "just a job to do" and nothing else and then I discover my deep alienation. If I really felt related to my world, really a part of it, I would not complain about dullness and boredom.

Uninteresting work confronts a monk with his unrelatedness, and it is in this confrontation that prayer can develop. If the experience of unrelatedness does not lead to prayer, it may lead a monk out of the monastery. In prayer I can enter into contact with the God who created me and all things out of love. In prayer I can find a new sense of belonging since it is there that I am most related.

Manual work indeed unmasks my illusions. It shows how I am constantly looking for interesting, exciting, distracting activities to keep my mind busy and away from the confrontation with my nakedness, powerlessness, mortality, and weakness. Dull work at least opens up my basic defenselessness and makes me more vulnerable. I hope and pray that this new vulnerability will not make me fearful or angry, but instead, open to the gifts of God's grace.

Thursday, 5

To become a permanent resident of the U.S.A., I have to prove that I am not a communist and that I have no syphilis. For the first, I have to be interviewed; for the second, my blood has to be analyzed.

This afternoon I was in Batavia, the nearest town of any importance, for the blood test. Everyone was pleasant, friendly, and very co-operative. Tomorrow I have to return for the results at the county building where my blood is being given the Wassermann test. It was a refreshing ride. I picked up two teen-age hitchhikers on their way home from football practice. "School starts tomorrow," they said. It is strange to hear people talk about going back to school while for me it is still four months away. I can't remember one semester since I was six years old when I was not in school as student or teacher. This will be my first real schooltime when school will mean *schola:* "free time."

Saturday, 7

In the afternoon, I had to drive the backhoe. I learned how to raise and lower the large bucket and how to scoop with it. When I drove the big machine back to the garage, I did not realize that its boom was too high to pass under the garage door which had not been raised all the way up. Suddenly I heard a loud cracking noise and when I turned around, I saw that I had given the lower part of the garage door much more than a bruise.

Brother Michael saw it all happening. As always, he kept smiling and said that this reminded him of the text of Revelations: "The tail of the dragon swept the stars from the heavens." With a twinkle in his eye he added, "Events like this always help me to remember the Bible better." With that consolation I went home and forgot about it quickly.

Tomorrow back to Connecticut to become a permanent resident in the U.S.A.

Monday, 9

At four o'clock I was back "home" in the Abbey. Friendly greetings met me from all sides. John Eudes came by and said, "Welcome home" and Brother Anthony wrote, "Good to have you back." I had been gone for twenty-six hours! It felt good to be missed, even for a few hours.

I am totally exhausted. Have a headache, toothache, I'm hungry, sleepy, and in a general state of disorder. But sleep and food will probably cure me soon. It is good to be back, and I am very happy to have more than three months left to be here.

Wednesday, 11

The short trip to New Haven has given me a very distinct feeling of starting the second half of my stay. Returning to the monastery truly felt like returning home. I realize how comfortable I feel here. I know the monks—and not only by name—I know the style of life, I know my way around, not only the house but also around the rules. The monks seem to feel at ease with me and consider me part of their life. All that sounds fine, but it is a real temptation, too. Somewhere I realize that the cozy feelings are not necessarily good for my spiritual life and that it will take a new conscious effort to keep my eyes on God and avoid settling comfortably in this house. I can collect around me many interesting and entertaining little activities, and slowly fill up all the empty space that the monastery offers me for being alone with God. Writing about prayer can become an excuse for not praying, responding to the different interests of the monks can become a reason for not really being alone. It will require special effort in the coming months to realize the fact that this is not my permanent home and never will be, even if I should stay for life.

In Abraham Heschel's *A Passion for Truth* I read today the words of the Kotzker (Rabbi Menahem Mendl of Kotzk): "He who thinks that he has finished *is* finished."[8] How true. Those who think that they have arrived, have lost their way. Those who think they have reached their goal, have missed it. Those who think they are saints, are demons. An important part of the spiritual life is to keep longing, waiting, hoping, expecting. In the long run, some voluntary penance becomes necessary to help us remember that we are not yet fulfilled. A good criticism, a frustrating day, an empty stomach, or tired eyes might help to reawaken our expectation and deepen our prayer: Come, Lord Jesus, come.

Thursday, 12

Silence. Indeed, silence is very important for me. During the last week, with a trip to New Haven full of discussions and verbal exchanges, with many seemingly necessary telephone conversations, and with quite a few talks with the monks, silence became less and less a part of my life. With the diminishing silence, a sense of inner contamination developed. In the beginning, I didn't know why I felt somewhat dirty, dusty, impure, but it dawned on me that the lack of silence might have been the main cause.

I am becoming aware that with words ambiguous feelings enter into my life. It almost seems as if it is impossible to speak and not sin. Even in the most elevated discussion, something enters that seems to pollute the atmosphere. In some strange way, speaking makes me less alert, less open, and more self-centered. After my discussion with students in New Haven last Sunday, I not only felt tired and strained, but I felt as if I had touched some-

thing that should not be touched, as if I had distorted
something simply by talking about it, as if I had tried to
grasp a dew drop. Afterward I felt restless and could not
sleep.

St. James really does not exaggerate when he writes:
"Among all the parts of the body, the tongue is a whole
wicked world in itself; it infects the whole body; catching
fire itself from hell, it sets fire to the whole wheel of creation. Wild animals and birds, reptiles and fish can all be
tamed by man, and often are; but nobody can tame the
tongue . . ." (Jm. 3:6–7).

St. Benedict is very clear about the importance of silence. He feels that silence is better than speaking about
good things. He seems to imply that it is practically impossible to speak about good things without being
touched by the evil ones too, just as it is virtually impossible to eat meat without killing. He writes: ". . . on account of the seriousness of silence, let permission to speak
seldom be given even to perfect disciples, though it be for
good and holy and edifying talk, for it is written: 'In
much speaking thou shalt not avoid sin' (Prov. 10:19);
and elsewhere: 'Death and life are in the power of the
tongue' (Prov. 18:21). For it is becoming to the master to
speak and to teach: to the disciple to be silent and to
listen."[4] Silence needs to become a real part of my life
when I return to school. "In much speaking thou shalt not
avoid sin." Many people ask me to speak, but nobody as
yet has invited me for silence. Still, I realize that the more
I speak, the more I will need silence to remain faithful to
what I say. People expect too much from speaking, too little from silence. . . .

Friday, 13

Talked with John Eudes. My main concern is related to
my awareness that three and a half months from now I
will be gone from here. I wonder about the influence of

this retreat on my future life. One desire is clear: to have a continuing contact with this community and its abbot. While I feel a great admiration, respect, and gratitude toward my fellow priests in Holland, they are too far away to fulfill my more intimate spiritual needs.

John Eudes considered my desire understandable, realistic, and meaningful and suggested that in the coming months I develop some ideas about my future life-style. What struck me most was his opinion that once I had made concrete decisions about prayer, availability, hours of rising and going to bed, and lived accordingly, my friends and students would support me and help me live this way. I would soon discover that those who are attracted to that life-style would want to join in it. In other words: A clear, visible, and well-defined life-style would give me a way of relating better to people and offer a criterion for my judgments in developing more or less intimate relationships.

John Eudes mentioned two possible points of concentration: the "Liturgy of the Hours" and meditation, and two possible times: early in the morning and before going to bed. He felt that recurring days of retreat would be really fruitful only when there was a daily discipline. Without a continuing rhythm of prayer, occasional or regular days of retreat would lose their connection with the rest of life.

We also discussed the importance of a better integration between prayer and work. Lecturing, preaching, writing, studying, and counseling, all these would be nurtured and deepened by a regular prayer life. John Eudes told me that Merton only wrote during "work hours" but had no problems finding ideas and subjects since it all seemed to flow easily from his prayer. He had two monks who worked for him as secretaries. One day they complained that together they could hardly keep up with Merton's daily output. But Merton himself did not feel he was forcing himself. What he wrote came easily and was part of his contemplative life. This is a "telling" story, and it holds important suggestions for me.

It seems crucial that I make clear-cut, concrete decisions and stick to them for a prolonged period. Then I should evaluate the experience with my director, make changes, try it again for a certain time, evaluate again, etc., until I have found a more or less permanent life-style, always open to changes but with a great deal of continuity. Both flexibility and continuity seem to be important aspects for a spiritual life-style in an active profession.

Theodore found a button among the raisins this morning. When he showed me the button, I thought of a poor Chicano who had been picking grapes in the hot sun of California and lost his button while carrying a full box to the truck. Today his button showed up in the raisin washing machine of a Trappist monastery. How good it would have been to be able to return the button with a big box of raisin bread for him and his family. But as always: The poor are and remain anonymous.

Saturday, 14

Monks go to a monastery to find God. But monks who live in a monastery as if they had found God are not real monks. I came here to come "closer" to God, but if I ever were to make myself believe that I am any closer to God than anyone else, I would just be fooling myself. God should be sought, but we cannot find God. We can only be found by him.

Two passages from Elie Wiesel's *Souls on Fire* about the Kotzker offer a powerful illustration of these paradoxes. In the first passage I read: "A disciple tells the Kotzker his woes: 'I come from Rizhn. There everything is simple, everything is clear. I prayed and I knew I was praying; I studied and I knew I was studying. Here in Kotzk everything is mixed up, confused; I suffer from it, Rebbe. Terribly. I am lost. Please help me so I can pray and study as before. Please help me to stop suffering.' The Rebbe peers at his tearful disciple and asks: 'And who ever told you that God is interested in your studies and your prayers? And what if he preferred your tears and your suffering?[5]

In the second passage it says: " 'Certain experiences may be transmitted by language, others—more profound—by silence; and then there are those that cannot be transmitted, not even by silence.' [The Kotzker.] Never mind. Who says that experiences are made to be shared? They must be lived. That's all. And who says that truth is made to be revealed? It must be sought. That's all. Assuming it is concealed in melancholy, is that any reason to seek elsewhere?"[6]

These passages have a Kierkegaardian quality. I can quite well understand that Heschel was struck by the parallel between the Kotzker and Kierkegaard. But there also is a mood that I find reflected in the early desert fathers. God cannot be understood; he cannot be grasped by the human mind. The truth escapes our human capacities. The only way to come close to it is by a constant emphasis on the limitations of our human capacities to "have" or "hold" the truth. We can neither explain God nor his presence in history. As soon as we identify God with any specific event or situation, we play God and distort the truth. We only can be faithful in our affirmation that God has not deserted us but calls us in the middle of all the unexplainable absurdities of life. It is very important to be deeply aware of this. There is a great and subtle temptation to suggest to myself or others where God is working and where not, when he is present and when not, but nobody, no Christian, no priest, no monk, has any "special" knowledge about God. God cannot be limited by any human concept or prediction. He is greater than our mind and heart and perfectly free to reveal himself where and when he wants.

Sunday, 15

After Lauds this morning, Tony Walsh, a Canadian who for many years was the director of St. Benedict Joseph Labre House in Montreal, spoke to the community. A very impressive man. He must be in his sixties, thin with very deep facial characteristics, simply—if not poorly—dressed, intelligent, witty, compassionate, warm, and catholic in the best sense of the word. He said, "The Gospel needs to keep its shocking effect. You can never claim to have fully understood the Gospel. It always should keep you on edge and never satisfied."

I was happy to meet this remarkable man. He suggested to me that one of the greatest temptations is to make the Gospel complex and so weaken its message.

Monday, 16

"When God prays, how would he pray?" Abba Arika [Rab], a celebrated sage who died in 247, suggested the following: 'May it be my will that my mercy may surpass my anger, that my mercy may prevail over my other attributes, so that I may deal with my children in the attribute of mercy and on their behalf stop short of the limit of stern justice.' "[7] We have always struggled to understand how God can be just as well as merciful. Indeed, the mystery of God is that he can be both to the highest degree. But *we* cannot. God's mercy does not make him less just. His justice does not make him less merciful. But *we* have to struggle to prevent mercy from becoming lack of justice, and justice lack of mercy. The pardon of former President Nixon by his successor, President Ford, is therefore quite understandably perceived by many as an act of grave injustice.

Tuesday, 17

This morning I put this question to John Eudes: "How can I really develop a deep prayer life when I am back again at my busy work? I have the tendency to finish small and large jobs as soon as possible, and as long as I remain surrounded by unfinished tasks, my prayer is nearly impossible since I use the time for prayer to wonder about the many things I still have to do. It always seems that there is something more urgent and more important than prayer."

John Eudes' answer was clear and simple; "The only solution is a prayer schedule that you will never break without consulting your spiritual director. Set a time that is reasonable, and once it is set, stick to it at all costs. Make it your most important task. Let everyone know that this is the only thing you will not change and pray at that time. One hour in the morning before work and a half hour before you go to bed might be a good start. Set the exact time and hold on to it. Leave a party when that time approaches. Simply make it an impossibility to do any type of work, even if it seems urgent, important, and crucial. When you remain faithful, you slowly discover that it is useless to think about your many problems since they won't be dealt with in that time anyhow. Then you start saying to yourself during these free hours, 'Since I have nothing to do now, I might just as well pray!' So praying becomes as important as eating and sleeping, and the time set free for it becomes a very liberating time to which you become attached in the good sense.

"In the beginning," John Eudes said, "your thoughts will wander, but after a while you will discover that it becomes easier to stay quietly in the presence of the Lord. If your head seems filled with worries and concerns, you might like to start with some psalms or a Scripture reading that can help you to concentrate and then you will be better prepared for silent meditation. When you are faithful in this, you will slowly experience yourself in a deeper way. Because in this useless hour in which you do nothing 'important' or 'urgent,' you have to come to terms with your basic powerlessness, you have to feel your fundamental inability to solve your or other people's problems or to change the world. When you do not avoid that experience but live through it, you will find out that your many projects, plans, and obligations become less urgent, crucial, and important and lose their power over you. They will leave you free during your time with God and take their appropriate place in your life.

It seems very convincing to me, even obvious. The only task left is this: simply doing it in obedience.

Wednesday, 18

It has become quite clear to me that my good plans for later will only be real if I start living accordingly now. Although I spent many hours in church, I had not yet set a special time for meditation. So I decided to make the time from 10:45 to 11:15 free for meditation. I had to interrupt other things to do it and realized how important it is to have this appointment with myself. Just sitting silently in church without anything to do while my mind is full of plans, ideas, and concerns is in itself an experience.

This morning I found it simply funny. I could see my thoughts running wild and getting nowhere. Indeed I heard myself say, "Since I am here for this half hour anyhow, I might just as well pray." I sensed the slow withdrawal of my nervousness, and the time went very fast.

One of the experiences of prayer is that it seems that nothing happens. But when you stay with it and look back over a long period of prayer, you suddenly realize that something has happened. What is most close, most intimate, most present, often cannot be experienced directly but only with a certain distance. When I think that I am only distracted, just wasting my time, something is happening too immediate for knowing, understanding, and experiencing. Only in retrospect do I realize that something very important has taken place. Isn't this true of all really important events in life? When I am together with someone I love very much, we seldom talk about our relationship. The relationship, in fact, is too central to be a subject of talk. But later, after we have separated and write letters, we realize how much it all meant to us, and we even write about it.

This is very real to me. When I think about prayer, I can talk about it with moving words and write about it with conviction, but in both situations I am not really praying but reflecting on it with a certain distance. But when I pray, my prayer often seems very confused, dull, uninspiring, and distracted. God is close but often too close to experience. God is closer to me than I am to myself and, therefore, no subject for feelings or thoughts.

I wonder if in this sense I am not participating in what the apostles experienced. When Jesus was with them, they could not fully realize or understand what was happening. Only after he had left did they sense, feel, and understand how close he really had been to them. Their experience after the resurrection became the basis for their expectation.

Thursday, 19

Today I had the strong feeling that things are basically quite simple. If I could love God with all my heart, all my soul, and all my mind, I would feel a great inner freedom, great enough to embrace all that exists, great enough also to prevent little events from making me lose heart. During a few hours I felt that the presence of God was so obvious and my love for him so central that all the complexities of existence seemed to unite in one point and become very simple and clear. When my heart is undivided, my mind

only concerned about God, my soul full of his love, everything comes together into one perspective and nothing remains excluded. I felt the great difference between single-
mindedness and narrow-mindedness. For the first time
I sensed a real single-mindedness; my mind seemed to expand and to be able to receive endlessly more than when
I feel divided and confused. When all attention is on him
who is my Creator, my Redeemer, and my Sanctifier, I
can see all human life—joyful as well as painful—and all of
creation united in his love. Then I even wonder why I
was so tormented and anxious, so guilt-ridden and restless,
so hurried and impatient. All these pains seemed false
pains, resulting from not seeing, not hearing, and not understanding. The real pain is the pain that I find in God,
who allowed all of earth's suffering to enter into his divine
intimacy. The experience of God's presence is not void of
pain. But the pain is so deep that you do not want to miss
it since it is in this pain that the joy of God's presence can
be tasted. This seems close to nonsense except in the sense
that it is beyond sense and, therefore, hard to capture
within the limits of human understanding. The experience
of God's unifying presence is an experience in which the
distinction between joy and pain seems to be transcended
and in which the beginning of a new life is intimated.

Friday, 20

Abraham Heschel reveals an aspect of spirituality in his
discussion of the Kotzker that seems practically absent in
Christian life and certainly has never been stressed in my
life. It is the aspect of protest against God. He writes:
"The refusal to accept the harshness of God's ways in the
name of his love was an authentic form of prayer. Indeed,
the ancient Prophets of Israel were not in the habit of
consenting to God's harsh judgment and did not simply
nod, saying, 'Thy will be done.' They often challenged
him, as if to say, 'Thy will be changed.' They had often

countered and even annulled divine decrees."[8] . . . "A man who lived by honesty could not be expected to suppress his anxiety when tormented by profound perplexity. He had to speak out audaciously. Man should never capitulate, even to the Lord."[9] . . . "There are some forms of suffering that a man must accept with love and bear in silence. There are other agonies to which he must say no."[10]

This attitude shows, in fact, how close the Jew, who can protest against God, feels to God. When I can only relate to God in terms of submission, I am much more distant from him than when I can question his decrees. Most remarkable, therefore, is that this intimacy with God leads to a feeling that has never been part of my thinking but might be very important: Compassion *for* God.

Heschel tells the beautiful story of the Polish Jew who stopped praying "because of what happened in Auschwitz." Later, however, he started to pray again. When asked, "What made you change your mind?" he answered, "It suddenly dawned upon me to think how lonely God must be; look with whom he is left. I felt sorry for him."[11]

This attitude brings God and his people very close to each other, so that God is known by his people as the one who suffers with them.

Heschel writes: "The cardinal issue, Why does the God of justice and compassion permit evil to persist? is bound up with the problem of how man should aid God so that his justice and compassion prevail."[12] The most powerful sentence of Heschel is: "Faith is the beginning of compassion, of compassion for God. It is when bursting with God's sighs that we are touched by the awareness that *beyond all absurdity* there is meaning, truth, and love."[18] This is an experience of deep mysticism in which active protest and passive surrender are both present, and man struggles with God as Jacob wrestled with the angel.

Monday, 23

Often I have said to people, "I will pray for you" but
how often did I really enter into the full reality of what
that means? I now see how indeed I can enter deeply into
the other and pray to God from his center. When I really
bring my friends and the many I pray for into my innermost being and feel their pains, their struggles, their
cries in my own soul, then I leave myself, so to speak, and
become them, then I have compassion. Compassion lies at
the heart of our prayer for our fellow human beings.
When I pray for the world, I become the world; when I
pray for the endless needs of the millions, my soul expands and wants to embrace them all and bring them into
the presence of God. But in the midst of that experience I
realize that compassion is not mine but God's gift to me. I
cannot embrace the world, but God can. I cannot pray,
but God can pray in me. When God became as we are,
that is, when God allowed all of us to enter into his intimate life, it became possible for us to share in his infinite
compassion.

In praying for others, I lose myself and become the
other, only to be found by the divine love which holds the
whole of humanity in a compassionate embrace.

Tuesday, 24

Yesterday I shared with John Eudes some of my
thoughts about prayer for others. He not only confirmed
my thoughts but also led me further by saying that compassion belongs to the center of the contemplative life.
When we become the other and so enter into the presence
of God, then we are true contemplatives. True contemplatives, then, are *not* the ones who withdrew from the

world to save their own soul, but the ones who enter into the center of the world and pray to God from there.

Wednesday, 25

Today I imagined my inner self as a place crowded with pins and needles. How could I receive anyone in my prayer when there is no real place for them to be free and relaxed? When I am still so full of preoccupations, jealousies, angry feelings, anyone who enters will get hurt. I had a very vivid realization that I must create some free space in my innermost self so that I may indeed invite others to enter and be healed. To pray for others means to offer others a hospitable place where I can really listen to their needs and pains. Compassion, therefore, calls for a self-scrutiny that can lead to inner gentleness.

If I could have a gentle "interiority"—a heart of flesh and not of stone, a room with some spots on which one might walk barefooted—then God and my fellow humans could meet each other there. Then the center of my heart can become the place where God can hear the prayer for my neighbors and embrace them with his love.

Thursday, 26

This morning—or this night—Brother Cyprian started to mix the dough one hour too soon. Most people tend to oversleep and start an hour too late, but Brother Cyprian suddenly discovered that instead of starting at 1 A.M., he had started at midnight. And since fermentation does not adapt itself to human errors, everything had to start an hour earlier. The bread went into the oven an hour earlier, came out an hour earlier, was sliced an hour earlier, and packed an hour earlier, and—because of a new rise in price—it also was labeled an hour earlier. So I was ready an hour earlier. But I felt a little off schedule and very tired during the afternoon.

Since I could not concentrate on my reading, I took a walk southward from the bakery and found Brother Alberic loading two railroad grain cars with wheat. Alberic had talked the railroad people into repairing an old railroad track that goes through the property. This made it possible to bring the cars very close to the Abbey to be loaded with grain. There was enough grain for at least four cars. It was an impressive view to see the golden grain pulled up in an auger and poured into the brand new, shiny, silver train hoppers. I climbed on the roof and peered in the large space. Thousands of bushels poured in. It is good to know that the Abbey has committed itself to use the money earned from grain for the hungry and poor in India, the Philippines, Nigeria, Peru, and other countries.

Saturday, 28

John Eudes' little three-year-old nephew was making joyful noises during Compline and was the first to run up to his uncle to be sprinkled with holy water. The monks let him go first and smiled when he got more water on his head than he had expected.

Sunday, 29

During his conference in Chapter this morning, John Eudes said, "Unless our prayer is permanent, our heart is not yet pure." That struck me as very meaningful. John Eudes stressed that not only liturgy but also spiritual reading and manual work are prayer.

St. Benedict sees as the three main aspects of the monastic life: *Opus Dei* (liturgy), *Lectio Divina* (spiritual reading), and *Labor Manuum* (manual work). All three form essential aspects of prayer. When manual work no longer leads us closer to God, we are no longer fully realizing our vocation to pray without ceasing.

How can manual work be prayer? It is prayer when we not only work with our hands but also with our hearts, that is, when our work brings us into closer relationship with God's creation and the human task of working on God's earth.

Spiritual reading also should be done from the heart. It should bring us into more intimate contact with God who reveals himself to us in Scripture, in the lives of the saints and in the reflections of the theologians.

When manual work and spiritual reading are no longer prayer but only a way to earn money or be intellectually stimulated, we lose purity of heart; we become divided and are no longer single-eyed and single-minded.

It is obvious that the simplicity that all this presupposes is not easy to attain. I find that my life constantly threatens to become complex and divisive. A life of prayer is basically a very simple life. This simplicity, however, is the result of asceticism and effort; it is not a spontaneous simplicity. It could be called a "second naïveté." The great saints are characterized by this "second naïveté" which is "willing one thing" (Kierkegaard) or "selling everything to buy the treasure you have found" (Mt. 13).

This morning I worked five hours in the bakery. First two and a half hours packing, then two and a half hours sticking price tags on the bags. It was very tiring and gave me a bad headache since I broke my glasses and could hardly see anything beyond a few feet. In any case, inflation feels real to me. Even my head feels inflated.

CHAPTER FIVE

OCTOBER
Strangers and Friends

OCTOBER

Wednesday, 2

Last week the distributor on whom the monastery is dependent suddenly raised the price of a loaf of Monk's Bread from $.55 to $.59. The monks had just received 500,000 plastic bread bags on which the old price was printed. The result is that for at least the next three months every bag has to be tagged with a label on top of the old price saying: "$.59." This morning I labeled a few thousand loaves which came out of the bagging machine. After a few hours of this dull job I felt numb as well as irritated. The thought that this sudden price rise would keep me labeling for at least a month did not especially help to restore my peace of mind. When I finally was replaced and walked away, hot from sweat and anger, I discovered that on the end of the same line on which I had been working, two monks were tagging other labels on the same bags saying: "Special Sale: $.53"! All upset, I said to Brother Benedict, "Why not just put on the special sale labels since that makes it two cents cheaper than the old price?" But Benedict, obviously understanding capitalism better than I, said quickly, "A reduction of two cents is not attractive to the buyer. The way it is now, we have a reduction of six cents. When people see that difference, they are more inclined to buy."

Meanwhile, hundreds of working hours were spent in raising and lowering the price on the same bag. Certainly a strange type of monks' work!

Finally, I wrote to Edwin Aldrin. It took a long time before I received his book *Return to Earth*, and it took also a long time before I had read it and was able to let it sink in. Aldrin's story of his trip to the moon with Neil Armstrong and Michael Collins is extremely revealing, not because of what it says about this great victory of modern technology, but because of what it says about the personal, more intimate experiences of the astronauts. The enormous competition and rivalry to be in line for this first moon walk, and the uncanny experiences afterward—traveling over the world and shaking hands with presidents, kings, and queens, as the man "who walked on the moon"—all against the background of a middle-class American family life, creates quite a story.

Aldrin's is a very honest book. Never have I seen such common human experiences described in the context of such an exceptional voyage. He writes about his depressions, his fears of speaking in public, his disorientation, his sexual problems, his psychiatric treatment, his conflicts with his wife, and, finally, his attempt to deepen his commitment to his family and to live a civilian life.

Few people are able to write successful books about their everyday family life. Yet Aldrin's story is of interest because it is set against the backdrop of his heroic journey into space. And so we learn more about the strange emptiness of the life of a modern family than about the moon.

I still have not been able to fully articulate what fascinates me so much in this book. In some way it seems to touch the essence of the crisis of our modern civilization. Maybe it is the strange absence of the spiritual, the numinous, the transcendent that is so alienating in this book. Although Aldrin, an Episcopalian, takes the Holy Communion in the spacecraft, his response to the whole enterprise seems strangely aspiritual. This becomes especially clear in the events after the trip. Aldrin has very little to draw from when the tensions are building up. He went to the moon. Now he has to go to the inner heart of life to prevent the moon from destroying him.

Thursday, 3

Tomorrow: the feast day of St. Francis of Assisi, a day that needs my special attention since I will need a lot of guidance to find an answer to the question, "What place does poverty really have in my life?" From a statistical point of view, I belong to the few very wealthy people of this world. I earn more money than I need. I have enough to eat, good clothes, a pleasant place to stay, and I am surrounded by family and friends who are willing to help when I have any problems.

Still, without a certain attempt to live a life of poverty I can never call myself a sincere Christian. Giving away all I have does not seem to be very realistic. First of all, I do not have many possessions, and giving away my money would simply mean becoming dependent on others, who have enough to worry about.

One form of poverty I have thought about is to adopt my monastic habit as a permanent form of dress, in this way eliminating the constant need for buying new clothes. Thus, I would also have the advantage of being easily recognizable by others as a man who desires to live a religious life and to keep himself from forms of living not appropriate to that desire. I talked it over with John Eudes during two meetings. At first, it seemed a good idea, but now it has become clear that in my work milieu, it simply would be an oddity and what seems a sign of poverty might just become an ostentatious way of being different. Now I feel as strongly about not having a monastic habit as I formerly did about having one. After John Eudes expressed his opinion that adopting this form of clothing was inappropriate the whole idea fell away from me and I could hardly believe that for a while it had taken such a central role in my thoughts about my future life-style.

Three aspects of poverty remain attractive to me: first, living a simple and sober life; second, not trying to be different from my colleagues in externals; and third, spending a good amount of time working with the poor and giving as much money as possible to people who are working to alleviate poverty. I hope that St. Francis will help me to discover how to make this concrete.

G. K. Chesterton writes in his book, *St. Francis of Assisi*, that St. Francis' argument for poverty was "that the dedicated man might go anywhere among any kind of men, even the worst kind of men, so long as there was nothing by which they could hold him. If he had any ties or needs like ordinary men, he would become like ordinary men."[1]

The idea that poverty makes a person free is of special interest in the context of the Senate hearings on Nelson Rockefeller, who wants to be confirmed as Vice-President. His wealth is there the main concern.

Friday, 4

Chesterton gives a beautiful insight into the conversion of Francis by describing him as the "tumbler for God" who stands on his head for the pleasure of God. By seeing the world upside down "with all the trees and towers hanging head downwards," Francis discovers its dependent nature. The word *dependence* means *hanging*. By seeing his world, his city, upside down, Francis saw the same world and the same city but in a different way. "Instead of being merely proud of his strong city because it could not be moved, he would be thankful to God Almighty that it had not been dropped."[2]

This conversion, this turn around, this new view made

it possible for Francis to make praise and thanksgiving his central attitude in a world that he had rediscovered in its most profound dependence on God.

Here, indeed, we reach that mysterious point where asceticism and joy touch each other. Francis, who was a very severe ascetic, is, nevertheless, known as the most joyful of saints. His joy about all that is created was born out of his full realization of its dependence on God. In fasting and poverty, he reminded himself and others of God's lordship. In his songs of praise and thanksgiving, he revealed the beauty of all that is obedient to its Creator.

Sunday, 6

Chesterton on Francis' compassion: "To him a man stays always a man and does not disappear in a dense crowd any more than in a desert. He honored all men; that is, he not only loved but respected them all. What gave him extraordinary personal power was this: that from the Pope to the beggar, from the sultan of Syria in his pavilion to the ragged robbers crawling out of the wood, there was never a man who looked into those brown burning eyes without being certain that Francis Bernardone was really interested in *him*, in his own inner individual life from the cradle to the grave; that he himself was being valued and taken seriously and not merely added to the spoil of some social policy or the names of some clerical document. . . . He treated the whole mob of men as a mob of kings."[8]

Tuesday, 8

This afternoon I washed quite a few rocks. The rock collecting phase seems to be over. The rock washing phase—scrubbing lime off the granite rocks—is now in full swing. Meanwhile, the church is starting to take shape. The main pillars are poured and the form of the church is becoming visible. It looks as if it is going to be a very intimate circle of monks and guests. My guess is that it is going to be a very meditative, quiet place that easily will invite prayer.

Friday, 11

Just before dinner Jay appeared. It was a great and happy surprise to see him. He had intended to come for a few days next week, but his plan to drive became impossible when his car was stolen, and so he took a plane to Rochester and hitchhiked to the Abbey. He will stay for a week and I hope that it will be a good stay for him. Jay is the first of my students to come to the Abbey. I discover in myself the desire to make him feel, see, and experience all I have done in the last four months, but realize that God touches each one in a different way. I hope at least that there will be enough quietude and silence for him to hear God's voice.

Sunday, 13

This morning John Eudes spoke in Chapter about autumn as a time of plenitude, a time of fulfillment in which the richness of nature becomes abundantly visible, but also a time in which nature points beyond itself by the fragility of its passing beauty. He started by reading Psalm 64, which speaks about the beauty of nature. He couldn't have chosen a better day to speak about this psalm. When I walked out I was overwhelmed by the beauty of the landscape unfolding itself before my eyes. Looking out over the Genesee valley, I was dazzled by the bright colors of the trees. The yellow of the hickory trees, the different shades of red from the maples and oaks, the green of the willows—together they formed a fantastic spectacle. The sky was full of mysterious cloud formations, and just as I walked down to the guesthouse, the sun's rays burst through the clouds and covered the land with their light, making the corn fields look like a golden tapestry.

The beauty of the fall is unbelievable in this part of the country. I can only say with the psalmist: "The hills are girded with joy, they shout for joy, yes, they sing."

Two weeks from now the colorful leaves will have whirled to the ground and the trees will be bare, announcing the coming of winter and snow. It will be only a few months before all the hills will be white and the green of the winter wheat covered with a thick blanket of frozen snow. But then we can remember the rich powers hidden underneath which will show themselves again to those who have the patience to wait.

Monday, 14

Thinking back on how I came to the ideas I have written down on paper, I realize how much they were the result of a constant interaction with people. I write against the background of my own history and experiences and others respond to me from their different histories and experiences, and it is in the interaction of stories that the ideas take their shape.

Someone might read what I wrote and discover something there that I myself did not see, but which might be just as valid as my original thought. It seems important to allow this to happen. If I were to try to prevent people from drawing "wrong" implications from my thoughts, I might fall into the temptation of thinking that I know what all the implications are. Maybe I should be happy that I do not know them. In this way, many people with quite different stories can move between the lines of my

hesitant ideas, opinions, and viewpoints and there create
their own. After all, people will never follow anyone's
ideas except their own; I mean, those which have developed within their inner self.

Tuesday, 15

Jay and I visited Brother Elias this morning. It was a
happy event. At 7:15 A.M. we walked together through
the woods to the hermitage. Nature was still waking up.
The clouds were heavy and the paths were covered with
the colored leaves pulled from the branches by the heavy
rain.

Elias welcomed us full of joy and with a sort of divine
excitement. After a short, silent prayer in front of his
chapel altar, we talked. Elias' eyes so eradiated the experience he talked about that Jay and I felt ourselves to be in
the presence of a holy man. "The Lord is so good, so good
to me," he said repeatedly and then he spoke about the
sun and the clouds, the rain and the winds, the wheat and
the weeds, the heat and the cold, all as great gifts of the
Lord given to bring Elias into a closer, more intimate contact with him.

There were laughter and smiles, tenderness and conviction, down-to-earth observations and ecstatic utterances
all flowing quite naturally from him but definitely revealing another world to us.

"Isn't the rain beautiful?" he said. "Why do we keep
resisting rain? Why do we only want the sun when we
should be willing to be soaked by the rain? The Lord
wants to soak us with his grace and love. Isn't it marvel-
ous when we can feel the Lord in so many ways and get
to know him better and better! He lets us experience his
presence even now in all that surrounds us. Imagine how
it must be when we can see him face to face!"

Jay looked at Elias, all smiles and joy. He felt that Elias
not only spoke about the Lord but spoke the Lord. Every

time Elias used the word "Lord," his whole body leaped with joy, and he was beaming with heavenly satisfaction. We spoke about many things: about Lebanon, where Elias' parents came from; about its hermit, Sharbel, whose beatification took place at the end of the Second Vatican Council; about Yoga, fasting, meditation, Scripture reading, books on saints, and many other things. But it all seemed like just one subject: how good the Lord is.

When Jay and I walked back to the monastery, we both felt grateful for having met this holy man. It even seemed that he had helped us come closer to each other.

Thursday, 17

This afternoon I drove Jay to the airport. He was happy about the week. The meeting with Elias had filled him with joy, and he felt it a great privilege to have met a man whose heart was so wide and deep that it could contain the beauty of people and nature.

At the airport we talked for a while, and it seemed as if a bitter spirit invaded me and compelled me to complain about the lack of response in people to whom I had offered gifts. I even went so far as to make it personal and told Jay how much I had regretted that he had not responded at all when I sent him an expensive book about which I was very excited. Jay pointed out that I obviously could not give without wanting something in return. He offered Elias as an ideal to strive for and said that my need for a response showed a basic insecurity. I became defensive in return and our discussion became trite.

How I wish that this had not happened. When I drove back to the monastery, I felt so depressed that I developed a headache and couldn't think about anything other than my own narrow-mindedness and lack of generosity. Why did I create such a petty atmosphere at the end of such a good week?

The only thing I can say now is that this incident

revealed mercilessly my vulnerability and showed me clearly how little it took to make me fall into very immature behavior. It even proved hard not to be defensive in my thoughts afterward. I hope that I can simply say that I am sorry and allow the wound to be healed by God, who showed me how little I had understood.

Thursday, 24

Busy day. At 4:15 A.M. I started working on the hot-bread line. The wheat bread came out of the oven so fast I couldn't get it on the racks and into the cooling room fast enough. Happily, John Baptist helped me out and prevented the bread from flying around. Meanwhile, I burned my arm on a hot pan. Stupid.

Theodore, busy with "feeding the oven," today celebrates the twenty-fifth anniversary of his entrance into the monastery.

This afternoon I worked in the creek collecting more stones for the church. The masons want large, heavy, granite rocks which they can still place as long as the roof is not yet completed. After that, the low-reaching roof will prevent the boom of the backhoe from setting the heavy rocks down on the right spot. We got about six huge rocks in the bucket of the Trojan. The heavy machine did well in the creek and Father Stephen maneuvered the "beast" carefully around the curves and between obstacles. We were proud of the "catch," and Joe, the head mason, showed great satisfaction but also made it clear that we had to wash the lime off before they could be used.

The altar, one large limestone block, was moved to its place today. Before the beams for the roof go up, the altar had to be placed. Too heavy and too large to be brought in later through the door. All went well with the large crane.

With all that heavy equipment and material the danger

of accidents remains real. Yesterday a beam fell on
Brother Quentin's left hand. Three of his fingers were
badly damaged. They "sewed him up" in the nearby
Health Center and gave him pain killers. I was amazed to
see him back and around as if nothing had happened.

Saturday, 26

Last night, this morning, and this afternoon I was part
of a retreat of twenty-five students from the Newman
Center of Geneseo State College. It is the first time since
May that I have given conferences or meditations. I used
a large wagon wheel to make the point that the closer we
come to God—the hub of our life—the closer we come to
each other, even when we travel along very different
paths (spokes). The wheel stayed in the center of the
room during the retreat.

The mood was warm, receptive, friendly, and gentle,
and I felt part of things. But I also was totally exhausted
when I went to bed last night at 11 P.M. More than ever,
I feel how much energy is required to speak. How hard it
is to speak from heart to heart about God and prayer. I
now realize how careful I have to be in accepting invitations to speak. If words have to grow out of silence, I will
need much silence to prevent my words from becoming
flat and superficial.

The remarks by the students about prayer were beautiful and full of meaning. Only they themselves did not
know it. When I went home last night, I thought, "What
do I have to say to these men and women who are so ear-
nest in their search for God and live such good lives?" But
then I realized that the only thing I have to do is to say
loudly what they already know in their hearts so that they
can recognize it as really theirs and affirm it in gratitude.

Sunday, 27

John Eudes spoke in Chapter this morning about the monastic vocation. The occasion was the celebration of the twenty-fifth year of monastic life of Father Bede, Father Francis, and Brother Theodore and the twenty-fifth year of profession of Brother John Baptist. Their dates were different but this day was set apart to celebrate them all.

One thought in John Eudes' conference touched me very much. He said that to respond to God's love was a great act of faith. He compared it to people who have felt very lonely and isolated, very rejected and unloved during many years of their life and who suddenly meet someone who cares. For such people it is very hard to believe that his or her care is authentic and honest. It requires a great act of faith to accept the love that is offered to us and to live, not with suspicion and distrust, but with the inner conviction that we are worth being loved.

This is the great adventure of the monk: to really believe that God loves you, to really give yourself to God in trust, even while you are aware of your sinfulness, weaknesses, and miseries.

I suddenly saw much better than before that one of the greatest temptations of a monk is to doubt God's love. Those who enter a contemplative monastery with the intention of staying there for life must be very much aware of their own brokenness and need for redemption. If the monastic life should lead them to a morbid introspection of their own sinfulness, it would lead them away from God for whom they came to the monastery. Therefore, the growing realization of one's sins and weaknesses must open the contemplative to a growing awareness of God's love and care.

During the Eucharist John Eudes spoke about the parable of the penitent publican. He made the observation that monks are not necessarily better or holier people than others. Instead, he said, they might very well be weaker and more vulnerable and come to the monastery to find the support of a community to enable them to be faithful in their search for God and to keep responding to his continuing love.

I was deeply moved by these thoughts. They had an unusual clarity and lucidity for me, and I felt very grateful that I was part of this community. I also realized that my coming here might well be seen more as a sign of my weakness than my strength.

During dinner we listened to the Fifth Symphony of Tchaikovsky. The music overwhelmed me by its powerful melodic streams and gave me a deep sense of joy.

Monday, 28

Last night my close friends Claude and Don arrived from Notre Dame. This morning I saw them at Lauds, and after my work with the hot pans, I showed them the bakery. They seemed tickled by my bakery suit and the unusual context in which they saw me. We had so much to share that we decided to wait with all our stories until 1975. They had traveled for the whole summer through Latin America, had had many new experiences in their teaching at Notre Dame University and many new plans for the future. And I had my five months of monastic experiences to talk about. So instead of using this three-day stay as an occasion to catch up with each other's story, we tried to make it into a real retreat experience.

It is very good to see my friends again and to make them part of my life, even though it is only for a few days. Our regular retreats together would become less deep if my experience here could not become to some degree their experience also.

Tomorrow morning we will spend some time with John

Eudes so that he, too, may become part of our constantly growing friendship.

Tuesday, 29

The meeting of John Eudes with Don, Claude, and me was very meaningful. We started by asking John Eudes about the political influence of monasticism, referring especially to St. Bernard's great political impact, and moved from there to a discussion of the meaning of monasticism.

John Eudes made it very clear that monasticism may have political, sociological, psychological, and economic implications, but that anyone who enters a monastery with these in mind would leave it soon. He described his own vocation as a response to his world, but a response in which God and God alone became his goal.

John Eudes described how the monastic life has three aspects: the *praktikos*, the ascetic practice; the *theoria physica*, a deeper understanding of the inner relationship of things; and the *theologia*, the mystical experience of God. By self-denial, such as fasting, obedience and stability, the monk learns to understand the forces of the world better and to look beyond them to God. John Eudes also explained the full sense of the classic saying that the Christian life consists of "fasting, almsgiving, and prayer." When fasting means self-denial, almsgiving means charity, and prayer the search for union with God, then indeed this short expression summarizes the life of the Christian.

John Eudes stressed that great politicians always are much more than tacticians. When you cannot look beyond tactics, you lose perspective, distance, and the vision to which you can relate your actions. That is why for Plato a politician had to be a philosopher.

Claude remarked that John Eudes was turning things upside down for him. While he in his studies was trying to add a religious dimension to politics, he noticed that John Eudes was stressing the importance of relativizing politics by pointing beyond it. Obviously, John Eudes and Claude were not in contradiction with each other, but the contrast in emphasis was apparent.

John Eudes did not deny the political implications of monasticism, just as nobody would deny the political implications of marriage. Even as a man and a woman do not marry because of the political character of the marriage institution, so no monk enters a monastery to be politically relevant. His single-minded interest is God and God alone.

I was very happy that Don and Claude had a chance to meet John Eudes and that, in this way, he became much more for them than someone I often talk about.

Wednesday, 30

This was a very tiring day. Working in the bakery, answering mail, talking with an old friend from Bolivia, spending time with Claude and Don.

It is good to realize how empty and fatigued I feel. Why? I don't really know. Probably because I am trying to keep the monastic atmosphere and unconsciously protest against all these interruptions. At one level, I feel I should not have so much mail and become so involved in people's lives; on another level, I feel I should. So there is the conflict. Instead of simply accepting the good interruption and enjoying it fully, I am holding back, saying to myself, "I really shouldn't be talking so much. I should be praying."

But still, all was very good and pleasant. The talks were far from "just chatting." They were exchanges on a deep personal level.

Thursday, 31

Before Don and Claude left, we had a meditation together. At Don's suggestion we reflected on Romans
12:3–21. After our days together, St. Paul's words had a
new and very convincing power for us. We had spoken
about personal renewal, about renewal of the religious
community of which we are part, and about being in but
not of the world.

St. Paul seemed to speak about all of this in the text we
chose: "Do not conform outwardly to the standards of this
world, but let God transform you inwardly by a complete
change of your mind. . . . Love must be completely sincere. Hate what is evil, hold on to what is good. Love one
another warmly as brothers in Christ and be eager to
show respect for one another. Work hard, and do not be
lazy. Serve the Lord with a heart full of devotion. Let
your hope keep you joyful, be patient in your troubles,
and pray at all times. Share your belongings with your
needy brothers, and open your home to strangers" (Rm.
12:2, 9–12).[4]

The words which seemed to summarize everything are:
"Do not conform outwardly to the standards of this world
but let God transform you inwardly by a complete change
of your mind" (Rm. 12:2).[5] We used the Phillips translation, which says: "Don't let the world around you *squeeze
you into its own mould.*"[6] We became aware during these
days of how much we had allowed the world to squeeze
us in and, therefore, had not created enough freedom to
let God enter into our innermost self and transform our
hearts and minds.

It was a good meditation that brought us very close to
each other and made us depart from each other with new
confidence.

CHAPTER SIX

NOVEMBER

Many Saints but One Lord

NOVEMBER

Friday, 1

Feast of All Saints. The readings, mostly from the Apocalypse, gave a glorious picture of the New Jerusalem. A city with splendid gates, full of beauty and majesty. We heard about the throne of God and the twenty-four thrones of the elders dressed in white robes with golden crowns on their heads. "Flashes of lightning were coming from the throne, and the sound of peals of thunder, and in front of the throne there were seven flaming lamps burning, the seven Spirits of God" (Rev. 4:5).

The whole day was full of glorious visions, glorious sounds and glorious spectacles, and it became clear that in this way we were presented with an image of the world to come.

During the day, however, I also read "The Week in Review" of the New York *Times* and was overwhelmed by the misery of this world. More and more it seems that dark clouds are gathering above our world: Asia, Africa, Latin America, Europe, the United States—all over the globe it seems that people are worrying about the dark forces that lead to hunger, war, violence, poverty, captivity and wonder if there is anyone who has the vision and the power that can offer hope for a better future.

I was deeply struck by these contrasting panoramas. How do they relate to each other? Where do they intersect and connect? The Church does not seem to be able to give much of a foretaste of the heavenly glory.

It seems that the vision of All Saints' Day remains "up in the sky," and that even sincere attempts to make it come closer by concrete changes in our present dark world are not very successful. All this made All Saints' Day a somewhat ambiguous feast.

Sunday, 3

"The monastery is the center of the world." This drastic statement by John Eudes in Chapter this morning reminded me of exactly that same statement made by Thomas Merton when he came to the Abbey of Gethsemani for the first time. The monastery is not just a place to keep the world out but a place where God can dwell. The liturgy, the silence, the rhythm of the day, the week, and the year, and the whole monastic life-style with the harmony of prayer, spiritual reading, and manual labor, are meant to create space for God. The ideal of the monk is to live in the presence of God, to pray, read, work, eat, and sleep in the company of his divine Lord. Monastic life is the continuing contemplation of the mysteries of God, not just during the periods of silent meditation but during all parts of the day.

In so far as the monastery is the place where the presence of God in the world is most explicitly manifest and brought to consciousness, it is indeed the center of the world. This can be said in humility and with purity of heart because the monk, more than anyone else, realizes that God dwells only where man steps back to give him room.

The many guests who come here all seem to sense this and feel more unified after their visit, even when it is a short one. Some even go home with the feeling of "having seen the Lord" and feel a new strength to face the struggle of everyday living.

Wednesday, 6

At 10 A.M. I had my weekly meeting with John Eudes. I asked him about my fatigue which keeps plaguing me every time I become involved with people. Especially after the retreat for the Geneseo College students, it was a real problem.

John Eudes said that I should accept this condition by taking the necessary extra sleep, but he also made it clear that it was definitely a psychosomatic situation. I put too much energy into any encounter, as if I have to prove each time anew that I am worth being with. "You put your whole identity at stake—and every time you start from scratch," John Eudes suggested. "Prayer and meditation are important here because in them you can find your deepest identity, and that keeps you from putting your whole self on the line every time you work with other people." He also told me that it is a proven fact that those who meditate regularly need less sleep. They are more at one with themselves and don't use others in their identity struggle.

We had talked about these things before, but today they had a new relevance for me.

Friday, 8

For the past few weeks we have had a Friday night lecture by a visiting seminary professor. He has been speaking about the doctrine of the Trinity and especially about the Holy Spirit. For me these lectures are a special experience.

What fascinates me about them is that they give me such a powerful sense of *déjà vu*. When I listen to them I feel as if I am back in the theological seminary. All the feelings I had then seem to return: I like the lectures, I am intrigued, I don't want to miss any—but at the same time I feel dissatisfied on a level I did not understand in the past but is now closer to my consciousness. After my ordination I was asked to continue to study theology. I asked the bishop to change that request and to let me study psychology instead. Somewhere I then felt that theology had left a whole area of my life experience untouched. I hoped that psychology would fill the need. It did so, although only very indirectly.

Listening to the lectures reawakened in me all my seminary feelings. I kept saying to myself, "How interesting, how fascinating, how insightful"—and at the same time I said to myself, "So what? What do all these words about God the Father, the Son, and the Spirit have to do with me here and now?" As soon as I step outside the circle of his terminology, which is very familiar to me, the whole level of discourse seems extremely alienating.

How do you speak about the Holy Spirit in such a way that it is clear and has something to do with my concrete life experience? I had that question in 1954, and now I find myself raising it again. But now I understand the question a little better.

Saturday, 9

The whole afternoon I tried to hammer large nails into a large beam. At a distance it always seemed so easy, but my nails had the strange habit of bending just before the head touched the wood. Standing on a platform, I tried very hard to get the "right swing." Michael explained kindly to me that I should not push the nail in the wood with the hammer but use "wrist power." I have the idea but not yet the technique. Of every four nails, one made it to the end. The others I clipped off with a big pair of scissors and then drove the rest into the wood, hoping that future generations would not see them.

But it was a pleasant afternoon. Quentin and Michael showed endless patience and broad smiles, and Ross, my fellow worker, consoled me with stories about his own hard beginnings. But he surely did better than I. Meanwhile, I found it all a welcome change from the rock collecting routine. If I get a few more chances at it, I might better my average for successful nails.

Meanwhile, the church is starting to take shape and you can feel a happy anticipation of the day when it will be ready for the monks to make it the center of their lives. In the liturgy today we celebrated the dedication of the Basilica of St. John Lateran in Rome. I am sure that more thoughts went out toward the new church here than toward the old basilica in Rome.

Monday, 11

This was a very flat day. Three hours on the hot-bread line, two hours answering mail, and three hours trying to make a reading list for next semester's courses.

In between I had a "debate" with John Eudes about Hitchcock's book *The Recovery of the Sacred*, which is read during dinner. I told him that I found it a "gossipy" book, pulling things out of context without a real sense for history, and basically narrow-minded, prejudiced, ultraconservative, and at times, offensive. John Eudes said that I overreacted, that the book only wanted to make the point that there had been a lot of irresponsible liturgical experimentation, a point worth making, and he stated that he enjoyed hearing it. He also said that he had been wait-

ing for my negative reaction, a remark which made me
angry.

Well—we went around and around and got nowhere. I
disagreed with John Eudes' idea that I overreacted, and
he disagreed with my idea that he was biased in his sym-
pathies. So not much of anything happened. We closed
with some good laughs, and—in a certain sense—I did not
feel badly about having expressed these feelings, but I decided that it was probably better not to use his time or
mine for this sort of argument. It is tiring and, considering
the short time of my stay, not very helpful for anyone—for
John Eudes, the monks, or myself.

I now feel somewhat dizzy and sloppy. Better get some
sleep.

Tuesday, 12

To live a spiritual life is to live in the presence of God.
This very straightforward truth was brought home to me
forcefully by Brother Lawrence, a French Carmelite
brother who lived in the seventeenth century. The book
The Practice of the Presence of God contains four conversations with Brother Lawrence and fifteen letters by him.

He writes: "It is not necessary for being with God to be
always at church. We may make an oratory of our heart
wherein to retire from time to time to converse with him
in meekness, humility, and love. Everyone is capable of
such familiar conversation with God, some more, some
less. He knows what we can do. Let us begin, then. Perhaps he expects but one generous resolution on our part.
Have courage."[1]

"I know that for the right practice of it [the presence of
God] the heart must be empty of all other things, because God will possess the heart *alone;* and as he cannot
possess it alone without emptying it of all besides, so nei-

ther can he act *there*, and do in it what pleases, unless it be left vacant to him."[2]

Brother Lawrence's message, in all its simplicity, is very profound. For him who has become close to God, all is one. Only God counts, and in God all people and all things are embraced with love. To live in the presence of God, however, is to live with purity of heart, with simple-mindedness and with total acceptance of his will. That, indeed, demands a choice, a decision, and great courage. It is a sign of true holiness.

Wednesday, 13

"God indeed hears our prayers." This joyful thought and feeling has dominated the entire day, after an unexpected phone call from California.

In 1971 my dear friend from Los Angeles, Richard, had an accident that caused a growing back pain. While visiting me in Holland his pain grew to such a degree that he had to be hospitalized. When finally he returned to Los Angeles, the pain had hardly decreased. From then on his life seemed a long battle of coping with the pain that made him more and more an invalid. He underwent surgery, went to chiropractors, had acupuncture, saw a very competent neurologist on the East Coast, tried psychotherapy, sat in whirlpools, lay flat for weeks, tried to act as if nothing were wrong—and took an endless amount of drugs. Just two weeks ago he had written: "No good news —only shit—the pain gets worse and I am getting more and more depressed."

About a month ago I told Brother James about Richard and said, "Please pray for my friend. He needs your prayers badly. It is not just his back. There is much more that needs healing." James prayed. He even prayed aloud for "the man who needs our prayers" during Vespers one evening.

After Richard's last despairing letter, I wrote back: "I

pray for you—I really pray—and I am sure you will be better soon. I am even somewhat angry that you are not better yet." I usually don't write things like that to Richard since words like: God, Church, priest, prayer, Jesus, all tend to evoke anger, irritation, and hostility in him. But this time I simply did so.

This morning John Eudes put a note under my door asking me to call Richard. "It is urgent," the note said, "but nothing bad." I called at 10 A.M. Richard's voice was full of joy as he said, "For five days I have not taken a pill. I have never felt so good."

Then he told me what had happened to him. One of the older students in his seminar on Latin American history had told him, "I will cure you." Richard had laughed but went to her home where she told Richard to shout, wrestle, jump and do all sorts of things which you would not normally ask of a man with a bad back. After an hour, much of the pain was gone. Although there were still many discomforts, Richard felt like another person. He had been shouting the last few days so much that his voice seemed different. Hoarse, of course. He also had been jumping and doing a lot of "acting out" and he felt great. From his description, it seemed that his therapist is a very responsible woman who knows what she is doing and has been able to sense the core of Richard's problem. After several therapy sessions Richard was so excited about the success that he wanted to tell me the story by phone. Suddenly he was full of new plans: finishing his dissertation, going to Paraguay, etc., etc. Although I was very glad, I kept telling him not to give up if a setback should come.

After dinner I told James. He beamed all over with joy. I said, "Please don't stop. Keep praying for him. It is just beginning." He said, "You so seldom know if God hears your prayers, and I feel so good that he listened to my request." Then I saw him walk away and kneel in the chapel. Meanwhile, I pray with him that this time Richard will be able to start a new life in all respects.

Thursday, 14

With great interest I read Evelyn Underhill's *The Mystics of the Church*. In this book Underhill discusses in a very lively and incisive way the main mystical figures in the Western Church. It is one of the most convincing arguments for the Christian belief that the love of God lived in its fullest sense leads to a most selfless dedication to the neighbor. Underhill shows how, after living through the most ecstatic experiences, the mystics are frequently capable of unbelievable activity. Paul is the prime example, but Augustine, Teresa of Avila, Catherine of Siena, and many others show the same capacity. Mysticism is the opposite of withdrawal from the world. Intimate union with God leads to the most creative involvement in the contemporary world. It seems that ecstasies and visions are slowly replaced by a "steady inward certainty of union with God and by a new strength and endurance."[3] Although frequently experiencing "sudden waves of fervent feelings" in this often very active period, the mystic is "none the less calm and sober in his practical dealings with men."[4]

Friday, 15

The Jesus Prayer has been very important to me ever since I came here. During the first weeks of my stay in the Abbey, I read many articles and books about Hesychasm in which the Jesus Prayer plays such a central role.

In recent days, I have come to realize how strong the devotion to the name of Jesus also is in the Western Church. I knew about this devotion, but more in the sense of a romantic piety than in the sense of a real road to deep prayer.

St. Bernard of Clairvaux plays a central role in the devotion to the name of Jesus. In his fifteenth sermon on the Song of Songs he writes: "When I name Jesus, I set before me a man who is meek and humble of heart, kind, prudent, chaste, merciful, flawlessly upright and holy in the eyes of all; and this same man is the all-powerful God whose way of life heals me, whose support is my strength. All these re-echo for me at the hearing of Jesus' name."[5]

So the name of Jesus indeed becomes the summary and expression of all prayer. This is very beautifully expressed in "The Rosy Sequence" (*Jesu dulcis memoria*), a poem formerly ascribed to St. Bernard but now presumed to be by an unknown English Cistercian.[6] The first stanza says:

> The memory of Jesus is sweet
> giving true joys to the heart;
> but sweeter than honey and all things
> is His sweet presence.

Here I found again how the memory of Jesus makes him present and how his presence makes me remember him. In the prayer of the name of Jesus, the memory and presence of God become one and the same and lead us into intimate union with him.

Monday, 18

What do you do when you are a monk and everyone around you is in the playful habit of cursing when something doesn't go as expected? This is no theoretical question since this is the case at the church building site where monks work closely together with good-natured and good-cursing workers.

I wondered how *I* would react. Probably I would not say anything but slowly get angry until I finally exploded and said, "Don't you know you are not supposed to curse!" Then we would all be angry, the air would be tense, and charity hard to find.

Well—Anthony told me *his* response. After having heard the name of Jesus used "in vain" (without effect—fruitless), he thought, "Should I say something about it?" He said to himself, "Why not?" Then the next time someone dropped a beam or bent a nail and used the name of the Lord again "without effect," he put his arm around him and said, "Hey, you know—this is a monastery—and we love that man here." The man looked up at him, smiled, and said, "To tell you the truth—I do too." And they both had a good laugh.

Having read so much about the Jesus Prayer and the power of the name of Jesus, this beautiful story has special meaning to me. Indeed, we should not use the name of the Lord in vain but only to bear fruit.

Tuesday, 19

I was struck by the following words in Henry Suso's *Little Book of Eternal Wisdom.* Jesus speaks: "Sometimes a clear eye is as quickly blinded by white flour as by gray ashes. Could the presence of any human being be more harmless than my presence among my beloved disciples? There were no unnecessary words, no unrestrained gestures, no conversations which begin with spiritual topics and end in useless babbling. True earnestness and complete, absolute truth dominated all our intercourse. Yet, my bodily presence had to be withdrawn in order to prepare the disciples to receive the Spirit. How great an obstacle, therefore, can human presence be. Before men are led into themselves by one person, they are drawn outward by thousands; before they are once taught with doctrine, they are many times confused by bad example."[7]

The world in which we live today and about whose suffering we know so much seems more than ever a world from which Christ has withdrawn himself. How can I believe that in this world we are constantly being prepared to receive the Spirit? Still, I think that this is exactly the message of hope. God has not withdrawn himself. He sent his Son to share our human condition and the Son sent us his Spirit to lead us into the intimacy of his divine life. It is in the midst of the chaotic suffering of humanity that the Holy Spirit, the Spirit of Love, makes himself visible. But can we recognize his presence?

Wednesday, 20

In my meeting with John Eudes today I asked him about total commitment to Christ. During the past few weeks I have often had a sudden insight into what that might mean. I have had a glimpse of the reality of being unconditionally committed to Christ, of a total surrender to him. In that glimpse I also saw how divided I still am, how hesitantly I commit myself, with what reluctance I surrender. I realized how totally new my life would be if I made Christ my only concern and at the same time how really "old" my life still is. I often say to myself, "I am very interested in Christ but also in many other things." That shows how uncommitted I am, how far from the experience out of which Henry Suso writes.

This probably explains also my fear of physical and mental pain. Reading about the torture to which so many people are subjected, I often wonder how long I could uphold my conviction under mental or physical pressure. I always end up with the realization of my weakness, lack of faith, and lack of unyielding commitment.

John Eudes pointed out to me that all these questions and concerns are part of the same problem. As long as I am plagued by doubts about my self-worth, I keep looking for gratification from people around me and yield quickly to any type of pain, mental or physical. But when I can slowly detach myself from this need for human affirmation and discover that it is in the relationship with the Lord that I find my true self, an unconditional surrender to him becomes not only possible but even the only desire, and pain inflicted by people will not touch me in the center. When my "self" is anchored not in people but in God, I will have a much greater resistance against pain.

We talked for a moment about torture and brainwashing, and John Eudes told me that in his psychiatric practice he had met a man who, as prisoner of war, underwent much torture but never gave an inch. He was a very simple, down-to-earth man with little political or ideological sophistication. But no pressure was able to force him to any kind of confession. John Eudes explained this by pointing to the man's sense of identity. No self-doubt, no insecurities, no false guilt feelings that could be exploited by his enemies.

How to come to this simplicity, this inner sense of self, this conviction of self-worth? "Meditate," John Eudes said, "and explore the small daily events in which you can see your insecurity at work. By meditation you can create distance, and what you can keep at a distance, you can shake off."

This led our discussion to a more profound question. If I allowed no one but the Lord to determine my identity, would I know the Lord? Or is it a fact that even in my meditation I relate to the Lord as I relate to people—that is—by manipulation and projection. Just as I can behave in my contacts with people in such a way as to provoke an affirmative response, so I can relate to the Lord on my own terms, thereby trying to make him like me. But then I am still more concerned with myself than with the Lord. Slowly I have to learn to meditate not on my terms but on his. Maybe I don't even know at all who the Lord is; maybe I have never allowed him to enter into my center and give me my real self, my identity. But when I discover the Lord on his terms, I will be able to let go of my own worries and concerns and surrender to him without any fear of the pains and sufferings this might lead to.

I see, I see—but when is God going to break through all

my defenses so that I can see not just with my mind but with my heart as well?

I have been moving lumber from the garage to the church. In June I helped put all the lumber into the garage; now I am helping to move it out. I had the feeling of coming full circle. It made me aware that I was not just working on the completion of the roof of the church but also on the completion of my stay here. Five weeks from now I will be in Holland and I will have to ask myself what these seven months have meant to me. I am still in it, but I see the end and the slow moving away to new experiences. During these months a church was built, a new space for God. Is this going to be true for me, too?

Friday, 22

André Malraux remarks in his *Anti-Memoirs* that one day we will realize that we are distinguished as much from each other by the forms our memories take as by our characters. I am wondering what form my memory is taking. It seems that this depends a great deal on myself. I have little to say about events, good or bad, creative or destructive, but much about the way I remember them—that is, the way I start giving them form in the story of my life. I am starting to see how important this is in my day-to-day living. I often say to myself; "How will I remember this day, this disappointment, this conflict, this misunderstanding, this sense of accomplishment, joy, and satisfaction? How will they function in my ongoing task of self-interpretation?"

Saturday, 23

The influence of Thomas Merton seems to have grown ever since he died in December 1968. Many people are writing masters' theses on him as well as doctoral dissertations. Books and articles on Merton keep appearing. Since I have been here, at least three books have appeared.[8]

One of the things that strikes me is that Merton is like the Bible: he can be used for almost any purpose. The conservative and the progressive, the liberal and the radical, those who fight for changes and those who complain about them, political activists and apolitical utopians, they all quote Merton to express their ideas and convictions. He is considered to be the man who inspired Dan Berrigan, Jim Forest, and Jim Douglas, but he also is used as "safe" spiritual reading in the refectories of many religious houses. Monks say that you cannot understand Merton when you do not see him primarily as a contemplative, while many non-monks prefer to see him as a social critic, a man living on the periphery of the monastery and deeply involved in the struggle for peace and justice. Christian admirers tend to stress Merton's orthodoxy, but many non-Christians who are looking to the Far East for new spiritual strength also claim him as their model and supporter. And although Merton, during his last days in Asia, wrote in the most unambiguous terms that he was and always would remain a Christian monk, some even want to believe that he planned to become a Buddhist.

What to think about this? Who is right and who is wrong? Merton never tried to be systematic and never worried about being consistent. He articulated skillfully and artfully the different stages of his own thoughts and experiences and moved on to new discoveries without worrying about what people made of his old ones. Now he is dead. He can no longer answer the question, "What did

you really mean?" He probably would only have been irritated by such a question. But his death has made him an
even stronger catalyst than he was during his life. He indeed made his own life available to others to help them
find their own—and not his—way. In this sense, he was
and still is a true minister, creating the free space where
others can enter and discover God's voice in their lives.

Sunday, 24

Today: the feast of Christ the King. No easy feast day
for me since I always have associated this feast with a certain triumphalism in the Church and with a militant spirituality, both of which were so much part of my pre-
Vatican II Jesuit formation. It also is the day in which I
am always confronted with the problem of authority in the
Church because it makes me realize how many people in
the Church like to play king in Jesus' name. Finally, it is
the day in which I have to deal with my own unresolved
struggle with obedience and submission, a struggle of
which I have again become very conscious in a monastery
such as this where the abbot is such a clear-cut authority
figure.

St. Benedict says in the Prologue of his Rule: "My
word, then, directs itself to you who have rejected the im-
pulses of your own will and have taken up the powerful
and splendid weapons of obedience in order to serve in
the army of the Lord Christ, the true King."[9]

These words leave no room for ambiguity. Christ is
King and therefore his will and not mine should be the ultimate criterion of my actions. Enough to start feeling
very uncomfortable. But today in the liturgy as well as
during my meditation, I started to see and feel that Christ
became our King by obedience and humility. His crown is
a crown of thorns, his throne is a cross. The soldiers knelt
before him saying: "'Hail, king of the Jews!' And they spat
on him and took the reed and struck him on the head with

it" (Mt. 27:30). While he hung on the cross, they said: "'If you are the King of the Jews, save yourself.' Above him there was an inscription: 'This is the king of the Jews'" (Lk. 23:36–38).

The great mystery of this feast is that we are asked to be obedient to him who was obedient unto the death on the cross, that we are asked to renounce our will for him who prayed to his Father: "Let your will be done, not mine" (Lk. 22:43), that we are challenged to suffer humiliation for him who was humiliated for our sake. Christ became King by emptying himself and becoming like us.

We are asked to be obedient to him to whom no human suffering is alien. How often do I say, think, or feel toward someone, "Who do you think you are to tell me what to do, to think, or how to behave?" When I say that to Jesus, he answers, "I am the Son of God who did not cling to my divine state but assumed the condition of a slave for you." (See Ph. 2:6–8.) The authority of Christ is an authority based on humility and obedience and received by experiencing the human condition in a deeper, broader, and wider way than any person ever did or ever will do.

This must make me realize that the kingdom of Jesus is "not of this world" (Jn. 18:36). It is not based on power but on humility, not the result of a revolt but given in response to obedience. It is in this kingdom that Jesus could receive the man who prayed on his cross: "Remember me when you come into your kingdom." "Today," the answer was, "you will be with me in paradise" (Lk. 23:43).

It is for this kingdom that St. Benedict wants to prepare his monks and, therefore, he presents them with obedience and humility as the way. It is the way which the King himself went.

The hard reality is that in our world humility and obedience are never totally separated from power and manipulation: We are challenged to see the will of God in people who are sinful like ourselves and always subject to using their authority more for the worldly kingdom, even when called Church, than for the kingdom of Christ. But

Jesus allowed the will of his Father to be done through Pilate, Herod, mocking soldiers, and a gaping crowd that did not understand. How little is asked of me. I am asked only to obey people who share my love for Christ and have often had a greater share in his suffering than I have.

But let me at least realize today that if I ever am asked to accept or exercise authority over others, it should be an authority based on a sharing in the suffering of those whom I ask to obey.

Monday, 25

More and more the hunger in the world is entering our consciousness. I have heard and read about it for years, but now it is the dominating issue. Without any doubt it is the question, the concern, the problem, and the challenge of the '70s. In the beginning of the '60s, civil rights occupied the center of our attention; at the end of the '60s the Vietnam War was the central issue. Now it is hunger, starvation, famine, death. It is an issue that is so enormous and so overwhelming that it is nearly impossible to grasp in all its implications. Millions of people are faced with death; every day thousands of people die from lack of food. It makes it all the more frustrating to think about this in a monastery where three days a week about 15,000 loaves of bread come out of the oven and where the wheat and corn harvest was better than in many previous years.

Thursday, 28

Thanksgiving Day is a most American day. It also seems to me the day which the people of this nation know how to celebrate best. It is a family day, a day of hospitality, a day of gratitude. It is the day that—unlike Father's Day, Mother's Day, and Christmas Day—has escaped commercialization. It is the day that makes me desire to be with a family here. It is the only day that makes me a little melancholic because in a Trappist monastery Thanksgiving cannot be celebrated in the traditional way. It is significant that the wine which was given to the monastery for Thanksgiving was used instead for the feast of Christ the King. Except for cranberry sauce—without turkey!—dinner had little to do with Thanksgiving. I keep wondering why monks don't seem to be interested in national feast days. I had expected Thanksgiving to be celebrated as a great feast, especially since it is the feast in which deep national and deep religious sentiments merge. But although Anthony had made a beautiful display of harvest grain and fruit under the altar, although Father Marcellus had us listen to Beethoven's Sixth Symphony during dinner, and although the Mass was the Mass of Thanksgiving, you could sense that the monks were not really celebrating as on Pentecost, on Assumption Day, or All Saints' Day. Maybe they resent the fact that the Pilgrims were not Catholics! Maybe, indeed, Thanksgiving is more a Protestant feast in history and character. Maybe it is just hard to celebrate Thanksgiving without your family.

Thanksgiving, however, is first of all a North American feast. This nation is affluent and has more than it needs. The realization that what we have is a free gift can deepen our desire to share this gift with others who cry out for help. When we bless the fruits of the harvest, let us at least realize that blessed fruits need to be shared. Otherwise, the blessing turns into a curse.

Saturday, 30

Vespers this evening opened the Advent season. A large green wreath with four candles, symbolizing the four Sundays before Christmas, was hung in the center of the choir. This simple decoration in the otherwise so sober chapel touched me deeply. Four weeks of expectation have begun. Expecting the day Christmas, expecting my final day in the Abbey, expecting my visit to Holland, and expecting my return to New Haven. It is good, very good, to have these weeks of expectations and to deepen my realization that all these small expectations help me come to a deeper awareness of the great day on which the Lord will return to fulfill his promises.

The expectation of Advent is anchored in the event of God's incarnation. The more I come in touch with what happened in the past, the more I come in touch with what is to come. The Gospel not only reminds me of what took place but also of what will take place. In the contemplation of Christ's first coming, I can discover the signs of his second coming. By looking back in meditation, I can look forward in expectation. By reflection, I can project; by conserving the memory of Christ's birth, I can progress to the fulfillment of his kingdom. I am struck by the fact that the prophets speaking about the future of Israel always kept reminding their people of God's great works in the past. They could look forward with confidence because they could look backward with awe to Yahweh's great deeds.

All this seems extremely important in a time in which our sense of history is so weak. Still it was the memory of the aspirations of the Founding Fathers, crystallized in the United States Constitution, which strengthened this country during the Watergate trauma and made it possible to regain some sense of national self-respect. Without anchors in its early promises and aspirations a nation is in danger of drifting and losing direction. And not only a nation, but the Church as well. It seems that progress is always connected with a refreshing of our collective memory. Practically all reforms in the Church and the Orders of the Church have been marked by a new appreciation of the intentions of the early Church and a renewed study of the past, not to repeat it but to find there the inspiration for real renewal. George Santayana once said: "Those who forget the past are doomed to repeat it."

I pray that Advent will offer me the opportunity to deepen my memory of God's great deeds in time and will set me free to look forward with courage to the fulfillment of time by him who came and is still to come.

CHAPTER SEVEN

DECEMBER

Waiting Quietly and Joyfully

DECEMBER

Sunday, 1

This first Sunday of Advent was a beautiful day and the liturgy made me constantly aware of the great expectation. I find myself singing a most beautiful Latin versicle which keeps welling up from my innermost being: *"Rorate coeli desuper et nubes pluant justum"* (You heavens send down your dew and let the clouds rain down the Just One); and the beautiful response: *"Aperiatur terra et germinet Salvatorem"* (Let the earth be opened and bring forth the Saviour). The strong supplicating melody keeps ringing through my head, and I see the divine dew covering the earth. God's grace is indeed like a gentle morning dew and a soft rain that gives new life to barren soil. Images of gentleness. My call is indeed to become more and more sensitive to the morning dew and to open my soul to the rain so that my innermost self can bring forth the Saviour.

Monday, 2

A heavy snowfall changed the scene today. There was a strong wind that made work outside practically impossible. The roof of the new church is still not finished and with this snow it is too difficult to work on such high, slippery places. Everybody hopes for another sunny week before the winter dominates the scene, but nobody can tell how great the chances are that this will happen. John Eudes returned late this evening from a retreat he gave in California. His plane had to land in Syracuse instead of Rochester, and it took him a long time to make it to the Abbey.

Tuesday, 3

"The grass withers, the flower fades, but the word of our God remains for ever" (Is. 40:8). The Word of God is powerful indeed. Not only the Jesus Prayer but many words from the Scriptures can reshape the inner self. When I take the words that strike me during a service into the day and slowly repeat them while reading or working, more or less chewing on them, they create new life. Sometimes when I wake up during the night I am still saying them, and they become like wings carrying me above the moods and turbulences of the days and the weeks.

In Isaiah I read: "Young men may grow tired and weary, youths may stumble, but those who hope in Yahweh renew their strength, they put out wings like eagles. They run and do not grow weary, walk and never tire" (40:30–31). The words of God are indeed like eagles' wings. Maybe I can deepen my hope in God by giving more time and attention to his words.

Once in a while I see a monk reading from a small pocket book of the psalms while doing something else (stirring soup, for instance). I know that he is trying to memorize the psalms. I recently read a letter written by a Trappistine sister in which she wrote that she knew more than half of the 150 psalms by heart. What a gift to be able to pray those words at any time and at any place. I can understand better now how they can give us eagles' wings and renew constantly our strength.

The words about God's coming not only remind us that God will appear, but also that he will slowly transform our whole being into expectation. Then we will no longer have expectations but be expectation, then all we are has become "waiting."

Wednesday, 4

Trudy Dixon, who edited *Zen Mind, Beginner's Mind*, writes concerning the special relationship between the Zen teacher and his student: "A roshi is a person who has actualized that perfect freedom which is the potentiality for all human beings. He exists in the fulness of his whole being. The flow of his consciousness is not the fixed repetitive patterns of our usual self-centered consciousness but rather arises spontaneously and naturally from the actual circumstances of the present. The results of this in terms of the quality of his life are extraordinary—buoyancy, vigor, straightforwardness, simplicity, humility, serenity, joyousness, uncanny perspicacity and unfathomable compassion. His whole being testifies to what it means to live in the reality of the present. Without anything said or done just the impact of meeting a personality so developed can be enough to change another's whole way of life. But in the end it is not the extraordinariness of the teacher which perplexes, intrigues and deepens the student, it is the teacher's utter ordinariness. Because he is just himself, he is a mirror for his students. When we are with him, we feel our own strengths and shortcomings without any sense of praise or criticism from him. In his presence we see our original face and the extraordinariness we see is only our true nature. When we learn to let our own nature free, the boundaries between master and student disappear in a deep flow of being and joy in the unfolding of Buddha mind."[1]

This beautiful description of the teacher-student relationship helps me very much to understand what the apostles must have experienced when they met Jesus and lived with him.

Thursday, 5

Today in Holland everyone is exchanging presents. St. Nicholas evening—the most playful, folkloric celebration of Holland. Full of surprises. The children are in the center, but nobody is excluded from attention. I miss it tonight. Many Dutchmen who are not in Holland will miss it also or will create their own St. Nicholas evening with other Dutchmen whom they gather together.

I am reading about a very non-Dutch idea: "In the beginner's mind there is no thought 'I have attained something.' All self-centered thoughts limit our vast mind. When we have no thought of achievement, no thought of self, we are true beginners. Then we can really learn something. The beginner's mind is the mind of compassion. When our mind is compassionate, it is boundless."[2]

I like these words. Also very important for Advent. Open, free, flexible, receptive. That is the attitude that makes us ready. I realize that in Zen you are not expecting anything or anyone. Still, it seems that all the things Shunryu Suzuki tells his students are important for Christians to hear and realize. Isn't a beginner's mind, a mind without the thought, "I have attained something," a mind opened for grace? Isn't that the mind of children who marvel at all they see? Isn't that the mind not filled with worries for tomorrow but alert and awake in the present moment?

Reading Shunryu Suzuki is like hearing far-away sounds which resonate in your innermost soul. They are far, they are close, they are strange, they are familiar, they are Buddhist sounds, they are Christian sounds. They are like the strange Magi from the East who were among the first to find the child.

Suzuki says: "After some years we will die. If we just think it is the end of our life, this will be the wrong understanding. But, on the other hand, if we think that we do not die, this is also wrong. We die, and we do not die. This is the right understanding."[3]

That is a sound coming from afar that resounds in my deepest self. It makes me recognize the words of the Man of Nazareth again, who left and yet remains, who died and yet lives, who came and is still to come.

Friday, 6

Sylvester told me today that he had received a postcard from Bob, one of my students who had spent a few days at the Abbey. He was beaming with joy and gratitude. This makes me realize how small signs of friendliness can create much joy and small disturbances between people much sadness while the "great events" of the day often do not touch us so deeply. An unexpected note from a friend or the passing remark from a neighbor can make or break my day emotionally, while inflation and recession, war and oppression do not touch my emotions directly. A distant catastrophe has less effect than a nearby mishap, and an interpersonal tiff raises more hackles than a world-wide calamity. The burning down of the monastery would be less "dangerous" than rivalry within its unharmed walls.

But how little do we use this knowledge? What is easier than writing a thank-you note, than sending a card "just to say hello," or to give a call "just to see how things have been." But how seldom do I do this. Still, I realize that every time someone says, "I liked your talk" or "I appreciated your remark" or "Your note really helped" or "You really seem to feel at home here"—I feel my inner life being lifted up and the day seems brighter, the grass greener, and the snow whiter than before. Indeed, the great mystery is that a small, often quite immaterial gesture can change my heart so much. The way to the heart always seems to be a quiet, gentle way. After Thanksgiving, I received a note from someone I do not know telling me how much she felt part of my life because of my writings. It seems that these are the most precious moments of life.

Sylvester's joyful eyes told me a story which I hope I'll never forget.

Saturday, 7

This year the Immaculate Conception of Mary the mother of God is celebrated one day before the official feast day. In this feast it seems that all the quiet beauty of Advent suddenly bursts forth into exuberance and exultation. In Mary we see all the beauty of Advent concentrated. She is the one in whom the waiting of Israel is most fully and most purely manifested; she is the last of the remnant of Israel for whom God shows his mercy and fulfills his promises; she is the faithful one who believed that the promise made to her by the Lord would be fulfilled; she is the lowly handmaid, the obedient servant, the quiet contemplative. She indeed is the most prepared to receive the Lord.

It seems that there is no better time to celebrate this feast than during these Advent days. It is the celebration of the beauty of her who is ready to receive the Lord. It is like admiring the palace where the King will enter, the room to which the bridegroom will come, the garden where the great encounter will take place.

I think of the painting on the ceiling of the Sistine Chapel where God stretches out his hand to Adam to call him to life. How beautifully humanity is created. Now God again is stretching out his arm to her who waits for his touch by which humanity is re-created even more beautifully. The celebration of this feast is the anticipation of the great event of Christmas. It makes me feel like a child on the evening before a wedding, full of joy and anticipation. I have already seen the bridal gown. I have already smelled the flowers. I have already heard the wedding song. There is no longer any doubt. Tomorrow it will surely happen; everything is ready to be fulfilled.

This feast day gives Advent its true character. It is indeed primarily a season of joy. It is not, like Lent, primarily a time of penance. No, there is too much anticipation for that. All-overriding is the experience of joy.

Sunday, 8

John Eudes said in Chapter that we should desire not only the first coming of Christ in his lowly human gentleness but also his second coming as the judge of our lives. I sensed that the desire for Christ's judgment is a real aspect of holiness and realized how little that desire was mine.

In his Advent sermon, Guerric of Igny understands that it is not easy to desire with fervor this second coming. Therefore, he says that if we cannot prepare ourselves for the day of judgment by desire, let us at least prepare ourselves by fear. Now I see better how part of Christian maturation is the slow but persistent deepening of fear to the point where it becomes desire. The fear of God is not in contrast with his mercy. Therefore, words such as fear and desire, justice and mercy have to be relearned and reunderstood when we use them in our intimate relationship with the Lord.

Monday, 9

The New York *Times* "Book Reviews" for December 1 gave a fascinating recap of the new books that appeared during 1974. Not only the articles but also—even more so —the advertisements gave a good impression of what keeps the minds of writers and readers occupied.

Among the hundreds of books announced, described, recommended, and criticized, very few are religious in nature. As a lonely dove among the many hawks, I saw the advertisement of *The Way of the Pilgrim* by Seabury Press. It says: "Now available in a beautiful slip-cased clothbound edition $7.50." I was thinking about the irony of this poor wanderer in Christ, whose only concern was to pray without ceasing, entering in this expensive dress into the competitive world of American publishers. But, except for the Russian pilgrim, most authors and their subjects represent different concerns. My impression is that most of the new books are looking backward rather than forward and are more about "those good old days" than about good new days. No doubt, a resurgent romanticism roams the land. Many books bring to mind forgotten treasures of former generations, help find the world's few leftover quiet spots, or reveal the simple life-styles of the past. Even their titles—*The Way Life Was, Farmboy, Times to Remember, The Last of the Nuba*—all suggest that there were better times and that there are better places than our time and place.

Seeing so many books displayed and discussed does not discourage me from writing. On the contrary, I feel a growing desire to enter into this world and to speak a word of hope. During periods of political or economic crisis, people tend to become more introverted and pensive. Sometimes books encourage a sort of collective daydreaming and create a world in which to escape. But they also can offer consolation and new strength. Hopefully, the readers of these books will gain a refreshed memory that will lead to new aspirations and new motivations to face reality now and to work in unity for a new world.

Tuesday, 10

On December 10, 1941, Thomas Merton entered Gethsemani. On December 10, 1968, he died in Bangkok. We prayed for him during Mass this morning.

I have been trying to make these last weeks in the Abbey weeks of special recollection. Sort of a retreat within a retreat. I did not want the last weeks to become weeks of packing mental suitcases but instead weeks of entering more deeply into the monastic experience. Advent helps very much. I have felt a great peace and inner quietude since Advent started. I am sufficiently used to the life and the people here to feel at home. I have not too much manual work to do, and what i do is routine work in the bakery or with the rocks. I have no strong desire to read great books or gather new materials and ideas. So I am quite free to give much attention to prayer, Scripture reading, and just a quiet way of living. At times, I feel a little guilty that I do not work more since everyone is so busy with the new church, but I realize that these guilt feelings are false and that I should not act upon them. At times, I want to delve into new books, but I realize that this is not the important thing to do and I let the idea pass as a temptation. I try to be quiet, to let the sense of expectation for the coming of the Lord grow in my heart and to simply enjoy being here and now.

Calmness, repose, even-mindedness, restful joy, gentleness: these are the feelings that describe best my present life. No great hostilities or disappointments, no great anxieties about leaving or fears about returning home. Nothing of that. No apprehensions, not even about the socio-economic or political future. I read the paper today and although last week proved in no way better than the weeks before, I did not feel deeply disturbed or restless. Most of the afternoon I carried slippery, snow-covered rocks into the church to be used for the inner walls. At times I thought that I recognized a rock I had picked up from the creek in June. I enjoyed it and felt friendly toward people and stones. I talked when I wanted and was silent when I wanted. It really didn't seem to matter very much. I feel very much at ease and still, and neither noise nor words nor actions seem to disturb this stillness. It is a grace-filled time and God is close.

Wednesday, 11

I had a very helpful session with John Eudes. When I told him that I felt deeply quiet, less restless, more prayerful, less compulsive, and freer, he said that if I had come to stay, this would have been the time to receive the habit of a novice. He was happily surprised that I could confirm the general experience that after six months the postulant is sufficiently at home to enter the novitiate.

I explained to John Eudes that I felt somewhat free from my compulsions. Normally, when I receive many letters I complain that I am too busy, and when I receive none I complain about lack of attention; when I work a lot I complain about lack of time to study and pray, when I work little I feel guilty for not making a contribution. In this sense I very much confirmed the vision of the French chaplain who, after fifteen years of hearing confessions, had learned two things: "People are not very happy and we never grow up."[4] But during the past few weeks I have felt an inner distance which has allowed me to *see* my compulsions and therefore to lose them, and I have experienced some new inner freedom.

John Eudes showed me how much my compulsive behavior could be seen as part of a way of being in which everything is experienced in terms of an "ought." I ought to be here, I ought to think such and such, etc. This way of being has many levels and touches many aspects of the personality. But when I am able to start seeing some of its symptoms from a certain distance and recognize them as symptoms of the "ought" compulsion, then I can slowly go all the way down to its roots and choose another way of relating to the world.

As John Eudes pointed out, the "ought modality" is closely tied up with the identity struggle. As long as I am constantly concerned about what I "ought" to say, think, do, or feel, I am still the victim of my surroundings and am not liberated. I am compelled to act in certain ways to live up to my self-created image. But when I can accept my identity from God and allow him to be the center of my life, I am liberated from compulsion and can move without restraints.

Saturday, 14

Last night Father van Torre from St. Bernard's Seminary in Rochester spoke to the monks. In his talk he used an illustration that I had heard before but that struck me suddenly as very revealing and convincing. When someone is very excited about the stained glass windows that Marc Chagall made for the synagogue of the Hadassah-Hebrew University Medical Center in Jerusalem, the only way to convince friends of their beauty is by bringing them into the synagogue.

This idea stayed with me the whole day because it convinced me more than ever of the importance of teaching spirituality from the inside. Next semester I will be fully occupied again with teaching. My task is not to make beautiful windows but to lead students into the synagogue where they can see the splendid colors when the sunlight shines through them. As long as students say that they are interested in spirituality but prefer to remain on the outside, no argument, enthusiastic description, or rich vocabulary will make them see what I see. Only by entering with me into the experience with which spirituality deals will any real learning take place. That does not mean that critical distance is not available and that subjectivity becomes the only criterion. On the contrary. Even from the inside we can step back and remain critical. Not everything we see from the inside is necessarily beautiful, worthwhile, or good. In fact, we are better able to make distinctions between bad and good, ugly and beautiful, appropriate and unfit from the inside than from the outside.

Does that mean that the only way to talk about prayer is by praying together? I don't think so. You don't have to be a Jew in order to be able to enjoy or appreciate the windows of Chagall, although as a Jew you will have a deeper understanding of their beauty than will someone to whom the Jewish religious tradition is unknown. But you have to enter into the world of the Jew, the synagogue, to enjoy its stained glass windows at all. In order to understand the meaning of prayer you have to be willing to enter into the world of praying men and women and discover the power and beauty of prayer from within. All this leads to the important question: How to introduce strangers into the world of prayer without forcing them into a kind of behavior that makes them feel uncomfortable?

Sometimes I am so excited about my new experiences here at the Abbey that I can hardly believe it when someone else does not share this excitement. But then, I have forgotten that I am shouting from the inside and that my shoulder-shrugging friends are looking at the same thing from the outside and wonder why I "exaggerate" all the time.

There is no doubt in my mind that it is worth my time and energy to lead my friends first to the inside of the building before I start trying to convince them of the beauty of the stained glass windows. Otherwise, I shall make a fool of myself by impatience and lack of ordinary educational insight.

Sunday, 15

Today is "Gaudete" Sunday, the Sunday to rejoice. For the entrance song of the Eucharist we sang the words of St. Paul: "Rejoice, again I say rejoice. The Lord is very near."

In Chapter John Eudes gave a beautiful meditation about this anticipatory joy. We are joyful already now because we know that the Lord will come. Our expectation leads to joy and our joy to a desire to give to others. Real joy always wants to share. It belongs to the nature of joy to communicate itself to others and to invite others to take part in the gifts we have received.

Advent is indeed a time of joyful waiting and joyful giving. John Eudes observed how much this mood is also part of our whole society. The period before Christmas has that remarkable quality of joy that seems to touch not only Christians but all who live in our society. When you, as a Westerner, live in another society, such as the Japanese society, where Advent and Christmas do not exist as universal events, you realize the lack of this joyful anticipation most painfully.

But Advent is not only a period of joy. It is also a time when those who are lonely feel lonelier than during other periods of the year. During this time many people try to commit suicide or are hospitalized with severe depression. Those who have hope feel much joy and desire to give. Those who have no hope feel more depressed than ever and are often thrown back on their lonely selves in despair.

Surrounded by a loving, supportive community, Advent and Christmas seem pure joy. But let me not forget my lonely moments because it does not take much to make that loneliness reappear. If I am able to remember loneliness during joy, I might be able in the future to remember joy during loneliness and so be stronger to face it and help others face it. In 1970 I felt so lonely that I could not give; now I feel so joyful that giving seems easy. I hope that the day will come when the memory of my present joy will give me the strength to keep giving even when loneliness gnaws at my heart. When Jesus was loneliest, he gave most. That realization should help to deepen my commitment to service and let my desire to give become independent of my actual experience of joy. Only a deepening of my life in Christ will make that possible.

Monday, 16

During my meeting with John Eudes today, I asked him if he had any ideas, observations, suggestions, or recommendations in regard to my stay here or my future life. In practically all our sessions over the last seven months I had set the tone and determined the subject of the conversation. Now I wondered if he perhaps had seen anything that I had missed or felt anything that needed to be expressed.

John Eudes felt that during the seven months we had talked about the most important things, and he did not feel that I had missed anything of special importance. But he felt it was crucial for me to find concrete ways to prevent myself from drowning in activities and concerns on my return home. We had often discussed my tendency to become overinvolved, to be carried away by sudden enthusiasm, to accept too many invitations, and to invest too much energy without considering whether or not it was worth it. If I want to maintain a steady prayer life and keep a certain purity of heart in the midst of all my actions, I need to set limits and find ways to say "no" more often.

I tried to formulate how I had come to see my own vocation more clearly during this retreat. Two things seem central: I am a priest and I am called to study and teach in the field of Christian Spirituality. Since I was six years old I have wanted to be a priest, a desire that never wavered except for the few moments when I was overly impressed by the uniform of a sea captain. Ever since my studies for the priesthood I have felt especially attracted to what was then called, "Ascetical and Mystical Theology," and all my other studies in psychology, sociology, and similar fields never seemed fruitful for me unless they led me to a deeper understanding of the questions of the spiritual life.

I have always moved from the psychological to the theological level and from clinical considerations to spiritual concerns. A sequence of courses—personality theory, clinical psychology, psychology of religion, pastoral psychology, ministry and spirituality, the history of Christian Spirituality, prayer and the spiritual life—seems to illustrate the movement of which I have always been part.

Where should my emphasis be now? It seems that my retreat has affirmed and deepened an already existing trend. What is becoming clear is the need to enter into both realities—the priesthood as a function and a life-style and the spiritual life as a field of special concentration—more deeply, more fully, more extensively, and in a more scholarly way. "Less speaking, more praying, more studying, and more writing" seems to summarize best the direction to take.

John Eudes strongly affirmed my self-evaluation. He felt that the direction I had pointed out seemed to be the way to go. He remarked that thus it would be much easier for me to maintain a spiritual discipline and refrain from spreading myself too thin. He also affirmed strongly the idea of combining more scholarly work in the field of spirituality with more long-term writing plans. He felt strongly that I should be more concerned with writing than with speaking, more with studying than with counseling, more with praying than with social life.

All of this makes me aware that I have entered into my

last full week at the Abbey and that the "termination process" has indeed begun.

Tuesday, 17

Richard wrote a letter saying: ". . . it is now over a month without codeine! Actually the pain is diminishing steadily. Yesterday I spent four hours driving. I have almost reached the point where I don't think of it anymore. The headaches are still a problem, but I am working on them. Have also been writing these past days. Looks like I am getting it together at that end, too."

This letter makes me leap for joy. After my intensive prayer in which I could nearly feel his painful back, after asking James for special prayers, and after recommending Richard to the prayers of the whole community, this letter sounded like music to me. I realize now how I really never doubted for a moment that God would hear our prayers and heal Richard very soon and completely, and also how grateful and joyful I was when he indeed responded so richly. "Not being surprised" and "being totally surprised" seems to have become one and the same emotion.

Richard has been very much in my thoughts and prayers since I received his letter. I have asked James and the whole community to continue in their prayers. I know how hard it is to allow healing to take place in our whole person—body, mind, and soul. But I also know that this is Richard's "hour," and that he has the strength to let go of his pains and open himself to others and the Other who reach out to him. Just knowing all this adds special joy to these final days here.

I moved rocks for three hours this afternoon and enjoyed it. The weather was mild and the mud not too bad.

Thursday, 19

During the last week of Advent it seems as if the lit-
urgy can no longer hide the excitement about the coming
of the Lord and bursts forth in anticipatory joy. During
Vespers the "O" antiphons express unrestrained exhila-
ration. "O Wisdom that proceeds from the mouth of the
Most High, O Adonai and leader of the House of Israel, O
Root of Jesse who stands as the ensign of the peoples, O
Key of David and Scepter of the House of Israel, O
Orient, Splendor of eternal light, O King of nations, the
One for whom they long, O Emmanuel, the Expectation
and Savior of the nations—come to us, O Lord, Our God."
Every evening between December 17 and 24 a new "O"
is sung and, slowly, waiting and welcoming, expecting
and seeing, hoping and receiving, future and present
merge into one song of praise to the Lord who has visited
his people.

What strikes me is that waiting is a period of learning.
The longer we wait the more we hear about him for
whom we are waiting. As the Advent weeks progress, we
hear more and more about the beauty and splendor of the
One who is to come. The Gospel passages read during
Mass all talk about the events before Jesus' birth and the
people ready to receive him. In the other readings Isaiah
heaps prophecy on prophecy to strengthen and deepen
our hope, and the songs, lessons, commentaries, and antiphons all compete in their attempt to set the stage for
the Lord who is to come.

There is a stark beauty about it all. But is this not a
preparation that can only lead to an anticlimax? I don't
think so. Advent does not lead to nervous tension stem-
ming from expectation of something spectacular about to
happen. On the contrary, it leads to a growing inner
stillness and joy allowing me to realize that he for whom I
am waiting has already arrived and speaks to me in the si-

lence of my heart. Just as a mother feels the child grow in her and is not surprised on the day of the birth but joyfully receives the one she learned to know during her waiting, so Jesus can be born in my life slowly and steadily and be received as the one I learned to know while waiting.

This last week is indeed a happy one.

Brian was hurt during work and will be in bed for quite a while. The bucket of the Trojan, loaded with stones, was lowered on the big toe of his right foot. The toe was smashed and the nail lost. Now he thrones in bed with a huge toe sticking out from under the sheets. The doctor told him: one week in bed and two weeks on crutches. Brian called it a "nuisance." With this understatement he put things in perspective. The pain is practically gone and he can read, write letters, and receive visitors. During the first day he had no lack of attention. During Lauds Brother Pat prayed for "Brian, who broke his toe."

Saturday, 21

Extra loaves and extra rocks. This morning 10,000 extra loaves were baked in the hope of conquering new "shelf space" in Cleveland. The distributor feels that the Abbey should expand the distribution of Monk's Bread because with the increase of prices, sales will drop off if limited to a small area. To give it a try all machines were turning their wheels today.

This afternoon we went back to the creek to pick up some heavy stones. The creek which was so quiet and sedate in June now looked like a small torrent. I had a hole in my right boot and the icy water found its way quickly to my shoe and foot. After changing boots with Brother Patrick who sat high and dry on the Trojan, I could help John Eudes better to push the rocks out of the water into the bucket.

At three o'clock I cleaned my room. Huge clouds of dust affirmed the fact that I had forgotten to clean it for three weeks. I got into a cleaning mood, threw every article of clothing that I could do without into the laundry, took a shower, combed my hair which had grown long enough again to be combed, put on a clean habit, and showed up in Vespers all shining. Four candles on the wreath were burning. First Vespers of the last Sunday in Advent.

Sunday, 22

This morning during Chapter John Eudes invited me to share with the community some of my impressions about my stay. He had told me a week ahead that he would do so, and I was happy to share with 'my brothers' my feelings of gratitude and joy.

Nevertheless, it is not easy to express in a few minutes experiences and emotions that are deep and often very broad. I ended up saying something about the Lord, something about the world, something about the brethren, and something about the saints. Let me try to write down the main content.

When I was a young child, my mother taught me the simple prayer: "All for you, dear Jesus." A simple prayer indeed but hard to realize. I discovered that, in fact, my life was more like the prayer: "Let us share things, Jesus, some for you and some for me." The commitment to serve the Lord and him alone is hard to fulfill. Still, that is the mark of sanctity. My life has always been sort of a compromise. "Sure, I am a priest, but if they don't like me as a priest, then I can still show them that I am also a psychologist, and they might like me for that." This attitude is like having hobbies on the side which offer gratification when the main task does not satisfy. The last seven months have revealed to me how demanding the love of the Lord is. I will never be happy unless I am totally, unconditionally committed to him. To be single-minded, to "will one thing," that is my goal and desire. Then also I can let go of the many pains and confusions that are the result of a divided mind. By allowing the Lord to be in the center, life becomes simpler, more unified, and more focused.

My stay at the monastery, however, has not only brought me closer to Christ, it has brought me closer to the world as well. In fact, distance from the world has made me feel more compassionate toward it. In my work in New Haven I am often so busy with immediate needs asking for an immediate response that my world narrows down to my daily worries, and I lose perspective on the larger problems. Here in the monastery I could look more easily beyond the boundaries of the place, the state, the country, and the continent, become more intimately aware of the pain and suffering of the whole world and respond to them by prayer, correspondence, gifts, or writing. I also felt that in this retreat my friends and family came closer to me. I experienced especially that a growing intimacy with God creates an always widening space for others in prayer. I had a real sense of the power of prayer for others and experienced what it means to place your suffering friends in God's presence right in the center of your heart.

But without the support of the community of brethren all this would have been practically impossible. My stay gave me a real new sense of community. When I experienced that I was accepted in the community, that my mistakes were hardly criticized and my good deeds rarely praised, that I did not have to fight for continuing acceptance, and that I was loved on a level deeper than that of successes and failures, I could come into a much deeper contact with myself and with God. God is the hub of the wheel of life. The closer we come to God the closer we come to each other. The basis of community is not primarily our ideas, feelings, and emotions about each other but our common search for God. When we keep our minds and hearts directed toward God, we will come more fully "together." During my stay in the Abbey I saw and experienced how many men with very different backgrounds and characters can live together in peace. They can do so not because of mutual attraction toward each other, but because of the common attraction toward God, their Lord and Father.

Besides communion with the brethren, I also discovered communion with the saints. In the past, the saints had very much moved to the background of my consciousness. During the last few months, they re-entered my awareness as powerful guides on the way to God. I read the lives of many saints and great spiritual men and women, and it seems that they have become real members of my spiritual family, always present to offer suggestions, ideas, advice, consolation, courage, and strength. It is very hard to keep your heart and mind directed toward God when there are no examples to help you in your struggle. Without saints you easily settle for less-inspiring people and quickly follow the ways of others who for a while seem exciting but who are not able to offer lasting support. I am happy to have been able to restore my relationship with many great saintly men and women in history who, by their lives and works, can be real counselors to me.

The words and questions after my short talk were very warm and sympathetic. John Eudes expressed his feeling that I had become a real member of the community even without vows or formal ties and hoped that the relationship that had developed over the past months would continue to grow in the future. That makes me feel joyful.

Tuesday, 24

In every respect a day of farewell. Many of the monks called me aside to say "good-bye" and to wish me well.

Anthony made some photographs of me. First he showed up at 3 A.M. in the refectory with his camera to "catch me" while eating breakfast. When I appeared at 4:15 A.M. in the bakery to work with John Eudes on the hot pans, Brother Anthony had his large lamp waiting for me there. He made some interesting shots—a few with Brother Theodore at the oven, a few with John Eudes at the cooling racks, and a few at the hot pans. He also took some photographs during Mass and finished his series of "monastic situations" with some more shots in the chapel and the library.

Meanwhile, the whole day was one of preparation. Benedict was busy cleaning the chapel. James and Joseph had their hands full with two Christmas trees. Gregory walked around with a great Star of David filled with light bulbs. Anthony tried to find the most artistic way to set up the Christmas scene under the altar. I just ran up and down with boxes, books, and clothes to get everything packed and ready before Vespers.

Everyone was in a playful mood, less serious than usual and more childlike. At 6:15 we sang Compline with a Christmas song at the start and now everything is quiet, very quiet for a few hours. I will try to sleep a little in the hope of being fully fresh and alert to sing Christmas Vigils and welcome God into this our suffering world so desperately in need of the Saviour. May his light shine in our darkness and may I be ready to receive it with joy and thanksgiving.

Wednesday, 25

How shall I describe this Holy Night? How shall I give expression to the multitude of feelings and ideas that come together in this most joyful celebration? This night is the fulfillment of four weeks of expectation; it is the remembrance of the most intimate mystery of life, the birth of God in an agonizing world; it is the planting of the seeds of compassion, freedom and peace in a harsh, unfree, and hateful society; it is hope in a new earth to come. It is all that and much, much more. For me it is also the end of a most blessed and graceful retreat and the beginning of a new life. A step out of silence into the many sounds of the world, out of the cloister into the unkept garden without hedges or boundaries. In many ways I feel as though I have received a small, vulnerable child in my arms and have been asked to carry him with me out of the intimacy of the monastery into a world waiting for light to come.

This day is the day in which I will experience not only the beauty of the night with songs of peace but also the wide ocean stretching out between two continents. This day the smallness and vulnerability of the child and the vastness of our earth will both enter my soul. I know that without the child, I have no reason to live but also that without a growing awareness of the suffering of humanity, I will not fulfill the call that the child has given me.

The monks smile and embrace me, the night is soft and quiet, the gentle sounds of the bells during the midnight "Gloria" still echo in my soul. All is still and quiet now. The branches of the trees outside are decorated with fresh white snow and the winds have withdrawn to let us enjoy for a moment the unbelievable beauty of the night of peace, the Holy Night.

What can I say on a night like this? It is all very small and very large, very close and very distant, very tangible and very elusive. I keep thinking about the Christmas scene that Anthony arranged under the altar. This probably is the most meaningful "crib" I have ever seen. Three small wood-carved figures made in India: a poor woman, a poor man, and a small child between them. The carving is simple, nearly primitive. No eyes, no ears, no mouths, just the contours of the faces. The figures are smaller than a human hand—nearly too small to attract attention at all. But then—a beam of light shines on the three figures and projects large shadows on the wall of the sanctuary. That says it all. The light thrown on the smallness of Mary,

Joseph, and the Child projects them as large, hopeful shadows against the walls of our life and our world. While looking at the intimate scene we already see the first outlines of the majesty and glory they represent. While witnessing the most human of human events, I see the majesty of God appearing on the horizon of my existence. While being moved by the gentleness of these three people, I am already awed by the immense greatness of God's love appearing in my world. Without the radiant beam of light shining into the darkness there is little to be seen. I might just pass by these three simple people and continue to walk in darkness. But everything changes with the light.

During these seven months the light has made me see not only the three small figures but also their huge shadows far away. This light makes all things new and reveals the greatness hidden in the small event of this Holy Night. I pray that I will have the strength to keep the light alive in my heart so that I can see and point to the promising shadows appearing on the walls of our world.

Now the only thing I can say on this Christmas morning, at the end of the event that started on Pentecost, is, "Thanks be to God that I have been here."

CONCLUSION

More than half a year has passed since I wrote the last entry in my Genesee diary. Rereading the many pages that I wrote during those seven months not only brought back to life many beautiful memories, but also confronted me with the present state of my heart and mind. Perhaps the greatest and most hidden illusion of all had been that after seven months of Trappist life I would be a different person, more integrated, more spiritual, more virtuous, more compassionate, more gentle, more joyful, and more understanding. Somehow I had expected that my restlessness would turn into quietude, my tensions into a peaceful life-style, and my many ambiguities and ambivalences into a single-minded commitment to God.

None of these successes, results, or achievements have come about. If I were to ask about my seven months at the Abbey, "Did it work, did I solve my problems?" the simple answer would be, "It did not work, it did not solve my problems." And I know that a year, two years, or even a lifetime as a Trappist monk would not have "worked" either. Because a monastery is not built to solve problems but to praise the Lord in the midst of them. I had known this all along, but still I had to return to my old busy life and be confronted with my own restless self to believe it.

Those who welcomed me back expected to see a different, a better man. And I had not wanted to disappoint them. But I should have known better. Using the monastery to develop a "successful" saintliness only makes me like the possessed man of whom Jesus says that "when an unclean spirit goes out of him it wanders through waterless country looking for a place to rest, and cannot find one. Then it says, 'I will return to the home I came from.' But on arrival, finding it unoccupied, swept and tidied, it then goes off and collects seven other spirits more evil than itself, and they go in and set up house there, so that the man ends up being worse than he was before" (Mt. 12:43–45). These words of Jesus have often entered my mind when old and new demons entered my soul. I hardly had an opportunity to think that seven months as a Trappist monk had cleansed my heart enough to be pure for the year to come. It took only a few weeks of being back to realize that I was having some troublesome visitors again. Without exaggeration I can say that some of my most humbling experiences took place after my return. But they had to take place to convince me once again that I cannot be my own exorcist, and to remind me that, if anything significant takes place in my life, it is not the result of my own "spiritual" calisthenics, but only the manifestation of God's unconditional grace. God himself certainly is the last one to be impressed by seven months of monastic life, and he did not wait long to let me know it.

Why did I go at all? Because there was an inner "must" to which I received a positive response. Why did I stay? Because I knew I was at the right place and nobody told me otherwise. Why was I there? I don't know fully yet. Probably I will not know fully before the end of the cycle of my life. Still, I can say that I have a most precious memory which keeps unfolding itself in all that I do or plan to do. I no longer can live without being reminded of the glimpse of God's graciousness that I saw in my solitude, of the ray of light that broke through my darkness, of the gentle voice that spoke in my silence, and of the soft breeze that touched me in my stillest hour. This memory, however, does more than bring to mind rich experiences of the past. It also continues to offer new perspectives on present events and guides in decisions for the years to come. In the midst of my ongoing compulsions, illusions, and unrealities, this memory will always be there to dispel false dreams and point in right directions. When Peter, James, and John saw the Lord in his splendor on Mount Tabor, they were heavy with sleep, but the memory of this event proved a source of hope in the midst of their later hardships. Maybe there can be only one Tabor-experience in my life. But the new strength gained from that experience might be enough to support me in the valley, in the garden of Gethsemani, and in the long dark night of life. The seven months at the Genesee Abbey might indeed have been enough to remind me constantly that now I see only "a dim reflection in a mirror," but one day I will see "face to face" (I Cor. 13:12).

REFERENCES

Chapter 1

1 Robert M. Pirsig, *Zen and the Art of Motorcycle Maintenance* (New York: Wm. Morrow, 1974), Chap. 17, pp. 211–12.

2 Ibid., Chap. 24, p. 286.

3 Larry Collins and Dominique Lapiere, *Or I'll Dress You in Mourning* (New York: Simon and Schuster, 1968), p. 104.

4 Henry D. Thoreau, *Walden, and Other Writings*, The Modern Library (New York: Random House, 1950), p. 290.

Chapter 2

1 *New York Review of Books*, May 30, 1974, p. 42.

2 Ibid.

3 Ibid., p. 38.

4 All psalms are quoted from *A New Translation from the Hebrew Arranged for Singing to the Psalmody of Joseph Gelineau* (New York: Paulist Press, 1968).

5 Dorothée de Gaza, *Oeuvres Spirituelles* in Sources Chrétiennes, No. 92 (Paris: Editions du Cerf, 1963), Par. 13, p. 145.

6 Ibid., Par. 66, p. 259.

7 Georges Gorree, *Charles de Foucauld* (Lyon: Editions du Chalet, 1957), Introduction.

8 De Gaza, op. cit., Par. 1, p. 307.

9 Ibid., Par. 94, p. 319.

10 *The Sands of Tamanrasset* (New York: Hawthorn, 1961), pp. 95–96.

11 De Gaza, op. cit., No. 5, p. 527.

12 Ibid., Par. 1, p. 307.

13 Diadoque de Photicé, *Oeuvres Spirituelles* in Sources Chrétiennes, No. 5 bis (Paris: Editions du Cerf, 1955), pp. 97–98.

14 See St. Bernard, "On Conversion," trans. and notes by Watkin Williams (London, 1938), p. 12 (Anchin Manuscript).

15 Ibid., p. 14.

16 *The Last of the Fathers* (New York: Harcourt, Brace, 1954), p. 52.

17 *The Cistercian Heritage*, trans. Elizabeth Livingstone (Westminster, Md.: Newman Press, 1958), pp. 72–74.

18 *U. S. News and World Report*, July 29, 1974, p. 41.

Chapter 3

1 Robert Jay Lifton and Eric Olson, *Living and Dying* (New York and Washington: Praeger, 1974), p. 116.

2 Thomas Merton, *Disputed Questions* (New York: Farrar, Straus & Cudahy, 1960), pp. 3–67.

3 Pasternak, *Doctor Zhivago* (New York: Pantheon, 1958), p. 335.

4 Murray Hoyt, *The World of Bees* (New York: Coward McCann, 1965), pp. 25–26.

5 *Conjectures of a Guilty Bystander* (New York: Doubleday, 1966), pp. 140–42.

6 Abraham Joshua Heschel, *A Passion for Truth* (New York: Farrar, Straus & Giroux, 1973), pp. xiv–xv.

Chapter 4

1 Theophan the Recluse in Igoumen Chariton, *The Art of Prayer*, ed. by T. Ware (London: Faber and Faber, 1966), p. 125.

2 Ibid., p. 131.

3 Heschel, op. cit., p. 87.

4 *The Rule of St. Benedict*, intro. and new trans. by Basilius Steidle, Eng. trans. Urban Schnitzhofer (Canon City, Colo.: Holy Cross Abbey, 1967), p. 112.

5 Elie Wiesel, *Souls on Fire*, Portraits and legends of Hasidic Masters (New York: Random House, 1972), p. 235.

6 Ibid., p. 240.

7 Heschel, op. cit., p. 131.

8 Ibid., p. 265.

9 Ibid., p. 269.

10 Ibid., p. 271.

11 Ibid., p. 303.

12 Ibid., p. 298.

13 Ibid., p. 201.

Chapter 5

1 Gilbert K. Chesterton, *St. Francis of Assisi* (New York: Doubleday Image Books, 1957), p. 101.

2 Ibid., pp. 74–75.

3 Ibid., pp. 96–97.

4 *Good News for Modern Man;* The New Testament in Today's English (New York: American Bible Society, 1966), p. 361.

5 Ibid.

6 J. B. Phillips, *The New Testament in Modern English* (London and Glasgow: Collins), p. 172.

Chapter 6

1 Brother Lawrence, *The Practice of the Presence of God* (Mount Vernon, N.Y.: Peter Pauper Press, 1973), p. 48.

2 Ibid., p. 43.

3 Evelyn Underhill, *The Mystics of the Church* (New York: Schocken Books, 1964), p. 43.

4 Ibid., p. 44.

5 *Bernard of Clairvaux*, On the Song of Songs I, Cistercian Fathers Series, Number Four (Spencer, Mass. Cistercian Publications, 1971), p. 111.

6 *Penguin Book of Latin Verse*, intro. and ed. Frederick Brittain (Baltimore, Md.: 1962), p. xxxi.

7 *The Exemplar: Life and Writings of Blessed Henry Suso*, O.P., Volume Two, intro. and notes N. Heller, Eng. trans. M. Ann Edwards, O.P. (Dubuque, Iowa, Priory Press, 1962), pp. 26–27.

8 Frederic Joseph Kelly, S.J., *Man Before God: Thomas Merton on Social Responsibility* (New York: Doubleday, 1974), Dennis Q. McInerny, *Thomas Merton: The Man & His Work*, Cistercian Studies Series, No. 27 (Washington: Consortium, 1974); Bro. Patrick Hart (ed.), *Thomas Merton—Monk: A Monastic Tribute* (New York: Sheed, 1974).

9 *Rule of St. Benedict*, op. cit., p. 57. Alterations in the translation are mine.

Chapter 7

1 Shunryu Suzuki, *Zen Mind, Beginner's Mind*, ed. Trudy Dixon (New York and Tokyo: Weatherill, 1970), p. 18.

2 Ibid., p. 22.

3 Ibid., on "Posture," p. 25.

4 From an interview with William Sloane Coffin, *Yale Alumni Magazine*, December 1974, p. 17.

Grateful acknowledgment is given for permission to quote material from the following sources:

Conjectures of a Guilty Bystander, by Thomas Merton, 1966,
Doubleday & Company, Inc. Copyright © 1965, 1966 by The
Abbey of Gethsemani; Quotations reprinted with the permission
of Farrar, Straus & Giroux, Inc., and Martin Secker & Warburg
Ltd. from *A Passion for Truth*, by Abraham Joshua Heschel.
Copyright © 1973 by Sylvia Heschel as Executrix of the Estate
of Abraham Joshua Heschel; "The Rosy Sequence" from *The
Penguin Book of Latin Verse*, introduced and edited by
Frederick Brittain, 1962, p. 220, Penguin Books Ltd. Copyright
© Frederick Brittain, 1962. Reprinted by permission of Penguin
Books Ltd.; The Grail's translations of Psalms 4, 78, 85, and 91
from *The Psalms: A New Translation*, published by William
Collins Sons & Co., Ltd., Collins - World and the Paulist Press
Inc., by permission of the Grail, England; *St. Francis of Assisi*,
by G. K. Chesterton, 1924, George H. Doran Company. Copy-
right 1924 by George H. Doran Company, by permission of
Doubleday & Company, Inc.; *Zen and the Art of Motorcycle
Maintenance*, by Robert M. Pirsig, 1974, William Morrow &
Co., Inc. Copyright © 1974 by Robert M. Pirsig; *Zen Mind,
Beginner's Mind*, by Shunryu Suzuki, edited by Trudy Dixon,
1970, John Weatherill, Inc.